T0339539

"Price and Evans have produced a ground-breaking, mind-altering book on how organisations and executives need to be thinking about and approaching information in their organisations, but why they regularly fail to do so. This perhaps is the most comprehensively researched and one of the most important books ever published on the topic of managing data as an actual enterprise asset and overcoming the persistent business pathology preventing it".

– Douglas B. Laney,
*Innovation Fellow, West Monroe Partners and
author of* Infonomics *and* Data Juice

"If you think money, people, and infrastructure, are your only assets to manage, think again. It is impossible to manage any other asset well without managing the data, information, and knowledge which underly them and are assets in their own right. Price and Evans offer compelling arguments based on experience, the latest research, and industry leaders. Learn from them and put this book to work!"

– Danette McGilvray,
President and Principal, Granite Falls Consulting, Inc. and author of
Executing Data Quality Projects: Ten Steps to Quality Data and
Trusted Information™, *2nd Ed. (Elsevier/Academic Press, 2021)*

"At a time when everyone seems to have become an instant data expert and AI genius, it's refreshing to read a rigorously researched and pragmatically laid out examination of this fundamentally important topic. In my view, it's a prime example of the Australian MBA culture (minimum bullshit allowed) in action and needs to be on everyone's reading list".

– Daragh OBrien,
*CEO, Castlebridge and Lecturer in Data Protection and
Data Governance, UCD Sutherland School of Law*

"Recognising data, information, and knowledge as assets and treating them as such may be the single most effective way a company can improve its strategic position. And doing so is an absolute necessity for those pursuing AI".

– Thomas C. Redman, *PhD*,
the Data Doc, Data Quality Solutions, Rumson, New Jersey, USA

Information Asset Management

Organisations are using data, information and knowledge as a competitive weapon. Their data, information and knowledge are arguably their most valuable assets. Yet, this fourth asset is managed badly when compared to the other three assets, namely money, people and infrastructure with considerable risk to the organisation. Executives are accountable for the success of their organisations, and those who don't manage this critical resource and business enabler effectively can be regarded as negligent.

Information Assets (IAs) carry enormous risk and value. Most boards and executives don't know how to govern and manage IAs effectively and nobody is held accountable. Given this, organisations should govern and manage their Information Assets the way they manage their Financial Assets. The benefits of managing IAs well are compelling. These benefits include increased efficiency, productivity, employee satisfaction, improved decision-making, mitigating business risk and improving product, protecting corporate reputation and service delivery. Drawing on ground-breaking research, this book explains why Information Assets are so important to organisations and the barriers to managing them well.

This book is unique in the sense that it takes a fresh look at this topic, is based on experience and research, and includes interviews from more than 70 industry leaders. In short, this book is written by executives and explains where to start.

Information Asset Management

Why You Must Manage Your Data, Information and Knowledge the Way You Manage Your Money

James Price and Nina Evans

Routledge
Taylor & Francis Group

A PRODUCTIVITY PRESS BOOK

First published 2024
by Routledge
605 Third Avenue, New York, NY 10158

and by Routledge
4 Park Square, Milton Park, Abingdon, Oxon, OX14 4RN

Routledge is an imprint of the Taylor & Francis Group, an informa business

ISBN: 9781032573885 (hbk)
ISBN: 9781032249711 (pbk)
ISBN: 9781003439141 (ebk)

DOI: 10.4324/9781003439141

Typeset in Garamond
by Deanta Global Publishing Services, Chennai, India

Contents

Preface

We have written this book for everybody who deals with data, information and knowledge. There aren't many people who don't. It is determinedly provocative and, we hope, challenging and uncomfortable. It challenges conventional wisdom and is based upon 15 years of our own research findings, including a quarter of a century of anecdotal evidence complete with project scars and commercially proven advice. Our research has been conducted over three continents with more than 70 C-level executives and board members. It is ethics-approved, peer-reviewed and published in highly ranked journals and conference proceedings. Ethics approval requires that identities are protected unless express permission has been granted to quote. Rest assured that every example and every quotation is from a real organisation or person. We have written this book to assist the reader to achieve their personal and corporate objectives and to achieve outstanding results. We have written it to inspire.

We hope this book is easily consumable, for example on a flight between Sydney and Melbourne. We have also tried to be practical and provide tools, including checklists, question sets and next steps that can be put into practice immediately. We hope that the book prompts you to take action immediately.

This book is about the effective governance and management of what are arguably an organisation's most valuable and vulnerable assets – its data, information and knowledge, i.e. its Information Assets. Managing Information Assets effectively does not have to be difficult and expensive. The General Manager of Wineries of a global wine company conducted a simple exercise to improve the management of a small winery's Information Assets. Without spending a single cent on computer hardware and software, the exercise was an unqualified success. Having improved productivity by over 10% and broken even on the project in eight weeks, the General Manager said to us, "There is no other project in our entire investment portfolio that could have delivered a greater result, more quickly, with better staff satisfaction". That is what we get out of bed for.

Despite the value and vulnerability of Information Assets, they are usually governed and managed badly. There are many reasons for this, but the most important is a lack of governance at both business and asset levels. In addition to a lack of governance, many organisations struggle to account for their Information Assets and the benefits that ensue from governing and managing these assets well. Both the Information Assets themselves and their resultant benefits are largely intangible. The International Financial Reporting Standard and the US's Generally Accepted Accounting Principles (GAAP) do not allow Information Assets to be capitalised and recorded on the Balance Sheet, making accounting for them difficult.

In our experience, organisations that have been successful in managing their Information Assets well are big enough to have a problem, yet are small enough to be able to deal with it. And they have someone who is passionate about driving business outcomes, who recognises that by managing their Information Assets well they can drive those outcomes and who is senior enough to impose lasting change.

As we see it, there are six states of Information Asset management awareness.:

1. There is no problem. Very few organisations are in this category. Even organisations of one or two people often can't find the information they need when they need it.
2. There is a problem, but the organisation is not aware of it. There is therefore no perceived need to address the problem.
3. There is a problem, and the organisation is aware of it, but there is no interest in addressing it. "We have an Information Asset Manager and we're all right, Jack". Or, "Crisis? What crisis? There is no crisis". Most organisations are in this category.
4. There is a problem, the organisation is aware of it and there is an interest in addressing it. Organisations in this category have enormous opportunities.
5. There is a problem, the organisation is aware of it and the problem is being addressed. Organisations in this category also have enormous opportunities but may run into difficulties.
6. There was a problem. In exceptional cases the problem has been recognised and it has been addressed and ameliorated. Very few organisations are in this category. We, the authors, are really interested in what has been achieved and how. Please contact us if you would like to share your experience.

Consider the following example. An evaluator of papers to a national conference of an industry association advised that Information Asset management does not appear to be, "novel or new to the oil and gas industry and [what you're telling us], the industry already knew and had demonstrated – many of the major oil and gas companies have Information Asset Managers". Spare me! Just because oil and gas companies have Information Asset Managers does not mean that they manage those assets as the vital resources they are. Our experience is that they don't. Not one of the mining, oil and gas companies we have worked with, and there are many, has been able to demonstrate to us that they manage their data, information and knowledge as a vital business asset.

Not convinced? Think about the following questions and answers.:

1	Question	How often do your Directors and Board members ask to see the Financial Statements, and the report on how well the organisation's Financial Assets are being managed?
	Answer	Every single Board meeting. Every single month.
	Question	And how often do they ask to see the Information Statements, the report on how well the organisation's Information Assets are being managed?
	Answer	The Board doesn't even know what they are.
2	Question	What would your organisation look like if it managed its Financial Assets with the same level of governance, accountability and corporate discipline as that with which it manages its Information Assets?
	Answer 1	An executive of a global oil and gas company said, "We would be broke in a week. Every person in this organisation would be able to spend any quantity of money for any purpose at any time without authority and without having to report on it because that's how we manage our information. The money would be walking out of here in wheelbarrow loads".
	Answer 2	Pointing to the floor, the Named Equity Partner of a Washington, DC-based law firm said, "Like that bloke there". "Like what bloke where?" "Precisely. Invisible. Non-existent. We would be out of business by Thursday".

Now that you have heard answers from executives, what would your answer to these questions be?

Effective deployment of Information Assets can help executives to improve business decision-making, mitigate business risk, reduce costs, drive substantial business value and benefit, and behave ethically. Because staff are being more efficient, effective and professional, they will be able to go home to their families on time with pride in their work. Yet, Information Assets are usually very poorly managed, preventing them from doing so, and injecting risk, waste and frustration. The result is that products and customer services are sub-optimal, organisations become uncompetitive or lose market capitalisation and/or their social licence to operate and their business results are not what they could be.

In the following pages we show that:

- organisations exist to deliver the right products and/or services to the people who want them at the right price and at the right time;
- they enable that by deploying and using the resources / raw materials at their disposal;
- the most successful organisations deliver the greatest value to their customers whilst consuming the fewest resources;
- data, information and knowledge are such critical resources; but
- typically, they are very badly governed and managed. We substantiate this claim with peer-reviewed research and real-life experiences;
- the reasons for their poor management fall into ten categories or domains, each of which is the subject of a chapter of this book;
- by investigating each domain, you create a picture of your Information Asset management practices and the business implications of those practices;
- at the end of almost every chapter we give you hard questions to ask of yourself and your peers; and finally
- we give you suggestions or next steps to proceed.

At the end of most chapters, we will challenge you (and encourage you to challenge yourself) by asking you a number of hard questions. These have been gathered over many years to highlight inconsistencies in how we govern and manage our vital business assets.

About the Authors

James Price has over 30 years' experience in the information industry and is internationally recognised as an author and presenter. He is the founder of Experience Matters, a firm that helps organisations protect and maximise the value of their data, information and knowledge, to address the problem that whilst Information Assets are vitally important to organisations, by and large they are very poorly governed and managed. His work with the University of South Australia as a lecturer and researcher has been described by Gartner, the world's most influential IT industry advisory firm, as "tremendous" and the research as "ground-breaking". Stuart Hamilton of Aquatic Informatics wrote, "I do believe that you have documented the greatest single barrier to productivity in the 21st Century economy and nobody knows about it".

James is passionate about:

- creating a business culture of professionalism, humility, teamwork, communication and laughter;
- helping clients drive tangible, measurable business outcomes from the efficient and effective management of their Information Assets; and
- giving back to the global Information Asset management community through his multinational research, publications and presentations, and his position as Chair of the Data Leaders Organisation (www.dataleaders.org).

Associate Professor Nina Evans started her career as a Chemical Engineer before completing a BSc(Hons) in Computer Science and a Diploma in Education and moving into higher education. Nina also holds a Masters' degree in Information Technology, an MBA and a PhD. She has worked as a lecturer, industry liaison manager, associate head of school, department head and vice dean. Nina is currently a Professorial Lead in the STEM academic unit of the University of South Australia (UniSA). In this role, she mentors academic staff, conducts research and teaches in the Master of IT program. In her teaching and research, she focuses on the interface between business and IT, information and knowledge management, holistic digital business transformation of both large and small businesses and ICT Leadership.

She has supervised PhD and doctoral students to completion and she has published 3 books and more than 100 papers in accredited journals and peer-reviewed academic conferences. Nina is passionate about university–industry collaboration and this book is the result of more than 12 years of working together to combine James' industry experience with Nina's academically rigorous approach to research. The collaboration is built on a relationship of trust in which "it is not about being right, but getting it right".

1

What Do Organisations Do and How Do They Do It?

INTRODUCTION

INTRODUCTION

In this chapter we will discuss:

1. what organisations do;
2. the assets and resources they deploy to conduct those activities;
3. why deploying these assets and resources efficiently and effectively is important;
4. governance and management;
5. intangible assets and their value; and
6. the need for a common language.

This chapter sets the foundations for the rest of the book. Understanding what the organisation does and how it does it is critical to deciding what resources are required for every business activity, every business process and every business decision.

EXECUTIVE OVERVIEW

The most successful organisations deliver the products and services that create the most value for their customers, whilst consuming the fewest resources. The assets and resources include its financial assets (money), physical assets (property and infrastructure including hardware and software), human assets (people) and intangible assets (which include data, information, knowledge, relationship capital, brand awareness and goodwill). An organisation's

DOI: 10.4324/9781003439141-1

governance and management dictate how its activities are conducted and its resources are deployed. Throughout this book, we will provide definitions and explanations to create precision of language and improve understanding of Information Asset governance and management.

WHAT ORGANISATIONS DO

Every organisation exists to meet its business objectives, which are dependent upon delivering value to its clients, whether they be in the commercial, government or not-for-profit sectors. Value is created for clients by the organisation delivering its product(s) and/or service(s) at an attractive price, of sufficient quality, in a timely manner. Products and services are created and delivered by conducting the organisation's business activities and processes, which are enabled by deploying its scarce and valuable resources (refer to Figure 1.1).

For example, an Australian consulting firm has nine major business activities as represented in Figure 1.2 comprising the following:

1. Primary activities, in the outer ring, which build capability and deliver services.
2. Support activities, in the middle ring, which provide the resources required to conduct the primary activities and are often referred to as Corporate Services.
3. Enterprise management, in the centre, which provides governance, strategy and planning.

FIGURE 1.1
What organisations do. (*Source*: Experience Matters.)

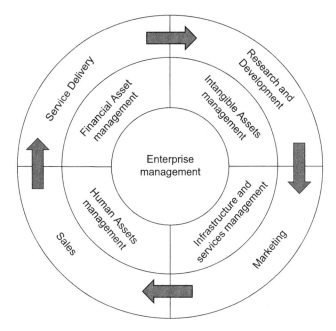

FIGURE 1.2
Major business activities. (*Source*: Experience Matters.)

THE ASSETS ORGANISATIONS HAVE

Oxford Languages defines an asset as "a useful or valuable person or thing". The current International Accounting Standards Board Framework defines an asset as "a resource controlled by the entity as a result of past events and from which future economic benefits are expected to flow to the entity". An asset can:

- be owned and controlled;
- be exchanged for cash; and
- generate future economic benefits for the owner.

The deployment of assets, particularly those that create competitive advantage, is espoused by Jay Barney, Richard Rumelt, et al. in the Resource Based View of the Firm theory (Figure 1.3).

If assets are positive, liabilities are negative. Liabilities are defined by Oxford Languages as "a person or thing whose presence or behaviour is likely to put one at a disadvantage". The International Accounting Standards Board has

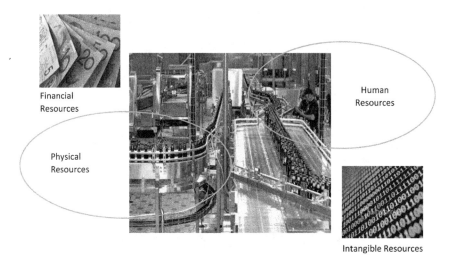

FIGURE 1.3
Factors of production. (*Source*: Experience Matters.)

tentatively defined a liability as "a present obligation of the entity to transfer an economic resource as a result of past events".

An asset becomes a liability when its potential benefit moves from being positive to being negative.

WHY DEPLOYING THESE RESOURCES EFFICIENTLY AND EFFECTIVELY IS IMPORTANT

Most senior executives think about:

- their corporate and/or departmental purpose, vision, mission, goals and objectives;
- the strategy they will implement to achieve those goals and objectives;
- what the organisation actually does, and the processes by which its business activities are conducted;
- the capability and capacity of the organisation as evidenced by the resources they have available through which they conduct those activities and processes;
- how they will govern, manage and deploy those resources to drive the greatest value and probability of success; and
- possibly the culture and language of the organisation.

When I am sitting on the beach on a hot summer's day in January, I think about how I will set my annual budget, what property and infrastructure I need to run the business, who will be on my team and what Intellectual Property we need to develop, maintain and extend our competitive advantage. For us, other than to keep the lights on, financial and physical assets don't matter. We are neither a bank nor a mining or transport company. What does matter is our team and the data, information and knowledge that they use to provide our expert advice and to help our clients drive business improvements and outcomes. If my most important management task is to make sure that our human assets are driving business, then isn't it my job as an executive to see that our "soldiers" are well equipped to take on the challenge? That's where data and information become our army's assets. We hope that this book will help equip both you and your team to drive business outcomes through effectively governing and managing your vital Information Assets.

As previously mentioned, the most successful organisations deliver the products and services that create the most value for their customers, whilst consuming the fewest resources. Let's be contentious. Contrary to conventional, accounting-based "wisdom", the job of management is not to drive business performance. The job of management is to deploy the organisation's scarce and valuable resources in the most efficient and effective manner possible and, if they are, then business performance will follow. Business performance is a lag, not a lead, indicator of good business management. It follows that the resources available to the responsible executive should be managed and deployed as efficiently and effectively as possible.

Associated with assets are risks, cost, value, benefits and ethics as per Table 1.1. These business impacts will be discussed further in Chapter 5.

GOVERNANCE AND MANAGEMENT

An organisation's governance and management dictate how its activities are conducted and its resources are deployed.

Governance refers to what decisions must be made and who makes those decisions to ensure effective management (executing the decisions).[1] John Ladley is a doyen of the Enterprise Information Management (EIM)

TABLE 1.1

Business impacts

Mitigate organisation risk		
• Access and security including cybersecurity	• Compliance	
• Disaster recovery	• Improved human safety	
• Business continuity	• Defence against competition	
• Litigation and discovery	• Personal and corporate reputation	
Drive benefits to the organisation	**Drive benefits to customers**	**Drive benefits to staff**
• Increased revenue	• Improved product and service development	• Better business decisions
• Reduced costs		• Safety of staff and contractors
• Profitability	• Improved product and service quality	• Faster activities and processes
• Productivity	• Faster delivery	• Reduced frustration
• Increased competitive advantage	• New products	• Improved staff satisfaction and morale
• Reduced mistakes & waste	• Reduced price	• Improved staff professionalism
• Reduced cost		• Personal reputation
• Social licence to operate		
• Higher shareholder returns		
Maintain business professionalism and ethics		
• Business integrity is achieved by acting impartially, ethically and in the interest of the business		
• Deciding, either actively or passively, to manage the business sub-optimally is arguably negligent		

(*Source:* Experience Matters)

industry and the author of numerous books and publications[2] including *Making EIM Work for Business – A Guide to Understanding Information as an Asset* and *Data Governance: How to Design, Deploy and Sustain an Effective Data Governance Program*. John says that governance is about oversight and control. It is about doing the right things.[3] Management refers to actually making and implementing decisions, particularly about the deployment of resources.[4] Management is about driving business value through execution. It is about doing things right.

There are (at least) two levels of governance, namely business governance and asset governance. Business governance provides oversight and control of the organisation as a whole, whereas asset governance provides oversight and control of specific asset types (financial, physical, human, intangible).

These are critical concepts that we will explore in detail in Chapter 7.

INTANGIBLE ASSETS AND THEIR VALUE

Oxford Languages defines an intangible asset as "an asset that can neither be seen nor touched" and "the non-physical assets of an enterprise such as patents, trademarks, copyrights, establishment expenses, and goodwill".

Doug Laney is one of the world's foremost authorities on Infonomics, the discipline of valuing data, information and knowledge as a strategic business asset. In his book, *Infonomics*,[5] Doug refers to the International Accounting Standard which defines the critical attributes of intangible assets as:

- non-monetary, lacking physical substance;
- capable of being separated and sold, transferred, licensed, rented or exchanged;
- subject to control, i.e. the right and power to use the asset; and
- having probable future economic benefit, e.g. revenue or reduced costs.

Intangible assets can include:

• intellectual property	• corporate culture	• brands
• patents	• employee innovation	• relationships with
• trademarks	• employee know-how	customers and suppliers
• data	• employee satisfaction	• customer lists
• information	• employee loyalty	• customer satisfaction
• published content	• training of employees	• customer loyalty
• knowledge	• relationships with	• distribution agreements
• strategies	investors	• supplier know-how
• organisational capabilities	• business reputation	• databases
• research and development	• corporate reputation	• management systems
• process quality	• product reputation	• technological processes

Note how many of these intangible assets consist of data, documents, content and knowledge, i.e. Information Assets. We will address Information Assets in Chapter 2.

Of the four sets of assets available to organisations, intangible assets are arguably the most valuable (Chart 1.1).

The world's economy is becoming increasingly service oriented and knowledge based. Work done by Ocean Tomo (2017) calculated that in 1975 intangible assets accounted for 17% of the Standard & Poor 500 (S&P500) companies' market value. The calculation is simple – Market Value minus Tangible Assets Value; the difference is the value of the organisation's intangible assets. This is significant, as the S&P 500 index consists of more traditional businesses, as opposed to the NASDAQ index which consists of mostly emerging, technology-based and data-driven companies.

In its "Intangible Asset Market Value Study" published in July 2020 Ocean Tomo shows that this number is now 90%. If we don't recognise that we are living in the knowledge economy, it's time we did.

Intangible assets now comprise the most valuable resource of most organisations. They deserve to be managed well. If a Board fails to govern, or executives fail to manage, protect and exploit, the organisation's most valuable asset, is that a good thing? Of course not. So, what should you do about it?

Michael Masterson, an intangible asset management specialist at Intrinsika, identifies the irony that most capital providers, companies and advisers focus on fixed assets with the result that most Boards, Directors and C-level executives do not understand:

- the intangible assets they own;
- the extent of the associated risks they face;
- the impact of intangible assets on financial results; and
- how to unlock value from their intangible assets and drive business performance.[6]

THE NEED FOR A COMMON LANGUAGE

A precise and common language is a business attribute that allows us to differentiate between ideas and terms, to finesse our message and meaning, to improve our comprehension, to avoid unsubstantiated assumptions and to reduce misunderstandings, thereby reducing mistakes and improving decision-making. In our interviews, one executive noted, "There is no standard language and glossary of terms. Outside of the organisation, but even within the organisation, it is a challenge to get everybody to speak the same language in terms of data governance and data management techniques".

As an example of precise and clear language, an Australian Defence organisation deeply understands the difference between a "boat" and a "ship".

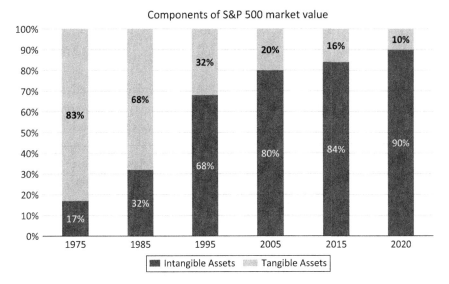

CHART 1.1
Market value of tangibles and intangibles. (*Source*: Ocean Tomo.)

A boat is a sub-surface vessel, a submarine, whereas a ship is a surface vessel like a frigate or a destroyer. It is important to get these differentiations right. On the other hand, an Australian university has four different definitions for the term "student commencement". One can imagine what confusion, inefficiencies, mistakes and rework such loose business definitions may cause.

Now that we've given you some food for thought, here's the first set of hard questions.

- What precisely does your organisation do and where is that clearly and concisely documented, i.e. on 1 page?
- What assets/resources do you deploy to run your organisation and to develop and deliver its products and services:
  - Financial assets (money)?
  - Physical assets (property, plant and equipment, IT)?
  - Human assets (people)?

  o Intangible assets?

  o Other?

- Within these types, which assets and resources are critical? Where is that documented?
- Within these types, which assets and resources are used in every business decision, every business activity and every business process?
- Within these types, which assets and resources cannot be replaced if stolen or lost?
- Which of these assets and resources are on the Asset Register?
- Which of these assets and resources are on the Risk Register?
- What governance, i.e. oversight and control, do you exercise over each of these asset types?
- What intangible assets does your organisation have:

  o Goodwill?

  o Brand awareness?

  o Relationship capital?

  o Information assets (data, information, content and knowledge)?

  o Other?

- What is the contribution made by intangible assets to the value of your organisation? How is that contribution calculated?
- If the most successful organisations are those that deliver the products and services that create the most value for their customers whilst consuming the fewest resources, how effectively does your organisation deploy these asset types to meet business goals. How is that measured?
- If you decide to govern and manage your organisation's assets badly, is that negligent?

NOTES

1. Evans, N. and Price, J. 2014. Responsibility and Accountability for Information Asset Management (IAM) in Organisations. *Electronic Journal of Information Systems and Evaluation (EJISE)*, 17(1): 113–121.
2. Ladley, J. 2010. *Making EIM Work for Business – A Guide to Understanding Information as an Asset and Data Governance: How to Design, Deploy and Sustain an Effective Data Governance Program.* Morgan Kaufmann.
3. John Ladley interview, 10th February 2022.
4. Khatri and Brown. 2010.
5. Laney, Douglas B. 2018. *Infonomics: How to Monetize, Manage and Measure Information As an Asset for Competitive Advantage.* Routledge: New York.
6. Michael Masterson presentation, 2022.

2

What Are Your Information Assets and Why Are They Important to You?

INTRODUCTION

In Chapter 1 we discussed:

1. what organisations do;
2. the assets and resources they have;
3. why deploying these resources efficiently and effectively is important;
4. governance and management;
5. intangible assets and their value; and
6. the need for a common language.

In this chapter we will:

1. define and describe Information Assets;
2. discover the value and vulnerability of Information Assets;
3. show how Information Assets should be governed and managed; and
4. differentiate between Information Assets and Information Technology.

Information Assets are the lifeblood of every organisation. They are required for every business activity, every business process and every business decision. They should be governed and managed well, but rarely are.

EXECUTIVE OVERVIEW

We define Information Assets as all data, records and documents, content and knowledge that are of value to the organisation. Information Assets

DOI: 10.4324/9781003439141-2

are arguably the most valuable of all the intangible assets. Without data, information and knowledge, no business activity can be undertaken, no business process can be conducted and no business decision can be made. The term "Information Asset Management" (IAM) refers to the processes and procedures used to deploy Information Assets to derive meaningful business insights and deliver those insights to consumers at the right time in the right format. Like other assets, Information assets have a lifecycle, and they are most cost-effective and deliver the greatest value if they are managed from their creation to their destruction.[1]

WHAT ARE INFORMATION ASSETS?

We define Information Assets as all data, records and documents, content and knowledge that are of value to the organisation. They can be found in:

- all media – paper, digital, film, head-space; and
- all formats – spreadsheets, email, drawings.

Information Assets are consciously deployable inputs to the decisions, activities and processes of the organisation and exclude:

- financial assets – money;
- physical assets – property and infrastructure including computer hardware and software;
- human assets – people;
- those intangible assets that cannot, or are difficult to, be consciously deployed – brand awareness, relationship capital and goodwill; and
- liabilities.

Information Assets can be classified, categorised and structured. In addition to the attributes of intangible assets, Information Assets also enjoy another, unusual attribute – they are not spent as other assets are and can be utilised without them disappearing. Indeed, they often become more valuable with use.[2]

We broadly categorise data, information and knowledge and is provided in Table 2.1.

TABLE 2.1

Data, Information and Knowledge

Data	Information		Knowledge
	Documents	Published content	
Structured	Unstructured		Unstructured
Explicit	Explicit		Tacit
Databases and application software	Boxes, compactus, library, media- and drives	Intranets and Internet sites	People's heads

The more we enrich our Information Assets with meaning and context, the more knowledge and insights we can drive and so we can make better, more informed decisions. This enrichment is sometimes referred to as the data to knowledge continuum and is explained in Table 2.2.

Whilst this table is the subject of some debate, it is useful to illustrate that there are differences between data, information, knowledge and wisdom. Tom Redman[3] points to Claude Shannon of Bell Laboratories who, in 1948, defined information on the basis of a reduction of uncertainty.[4]

Laura Sebastian-Coleman is the editor of the bible of data governance, DAMA's DMBoK, and is the author of *Navigating the Labyrinth* and *Meeting the Challenges of Data Quality Management"*. As Laura points out, it is very important to note that this continuum is neither linear, i.e. one state doesn't morph neatly into the next one, nor finite, i.e. knowledge can feed back into the quality of data. The scale assumes that data is the raw material and ignores that data is context dependent and requires knowledge and wisdom about what the data is telling us. Data also compresses information into codified form to make it more usable. The continuum therefore needs to recognise the circular and iterative nature of Information Assets.

All assets have a lifecycle. For instance, a ship is conceived, designed, built, commissioned, used, maintained, decommissioned and finally sunk or otherwise destroyed. Assets are most cost-effective and deliver the greatest value if they are managed throughout their lifecycle. Many physical assets are designed, built, maintained and decommissioned without reference to, or care for, the other parts of their lifecycle.

Some products and infrastructure are planned, designed and built without regard to their lifecycles, i.e. from initial concept through to decommissioning. This often results in considerable rework and expense. For example, in 2009 the

TABLE 2.2

Meaning and Context for Decision-making

State	Description	Examples
Data	Data are raw letters, numbers, pictures, etc. without context. Data may be stored in databases and processed by electronic manipulation, typically through application software. At this level, no explicit relationships among the data are obvious.	130890 are data
Information	Information comprises documents, records and both enterprise and web content. Information is data in context. Data becomes information when it has meaning and adds value for the user.	13/08/90 or 13 August 1990 is a date.
Documents, records and their management	A document is a container providing structure for information or evidence, stored on paper, digital or other form. It may be represented in multiple formats including content published as web pages. Where a document is used in the transaction of the organisation's business or the conduct of its affairs and needs to be kept as evidence of this activity, it becomes a record and subject to the rules and practices of records management. Document and Records Management focuses on controlling the lifecycle, i.e. the creation, capture, naming, storage, publishing, access, use, editing and reuse, archiving and ultimate destruction, of documents.	
Knowledge	In general terms, knowledge is belief, obtained through experience or association. It is comprised of an understanding of relationships between the facts and their implications. Knowledge is the applicability of associated facts within specific contexts.	My partner was born on 13th August 1990.
Wisdom	Wisdom is the consistently successful application of knowledge over time. The Oxford English Dictionary describes wisdom as "a body of knowledge and experience that develops within a specified society or period". It is knowledge gained, usually with life experience; it is gained awareness. It is a trait possessed by an individual, group or organisation.	It's wise to remember my partner's birthday. It is even wiser to buy her a present.
Judgement	According to the Oxford English Dictionary judgement is "the ability to make considered decisions or come to sensible conclusions". It is a subset of wisdom and often made with the benefit of experience.	You'll get it wrong. Take her with you to choose what she wants.

builders of a dedicated busway had to revert to the surveyors 22 times at a cost of $2,000[5] per day because what had been designed was inappropriate, and they were built without consideration of how they would be maintained. In another example, in 2001, when called to evaluate and rectify a problem in a substation, the engineers of a power transmission company couldn't trust the drawings of its substations and had to visit the site first to see what was actually there, again with considerable expense. It pays to take a holistic approach to the asset's life cycle.

It is the same with Information Assets. In Australia, financial records must be kept for seven years. Without a good business reason to do so, it is madness to keep them for longer than that. Most data and information are of poor quality – obsolete, duplicate, inaccurate, incomplete and/or irrelevant. Worse than just costing money and taking up space, it clutters the Infosphere making the information you want much harder to find. This in turn increases risk, increases cost, dilutes value and makes driving benefit from that data and information more difficult to achieve. It pays to take a holistic approach to an Information Asset's life cycle.

Information Assets have a lifecycle that is illustrated in Figure 2.1.

Planning, designing, managing and maintaining is a continuous activity; it's a golden thread that runs throughout the entire lifecycle.

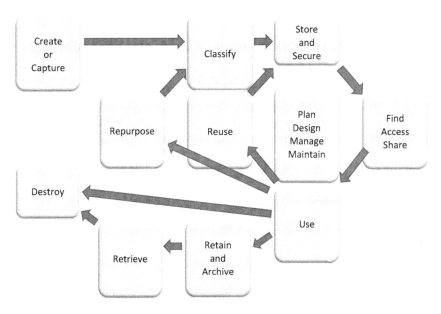

FIGURE 2.1
Information asset lifecycle. (*Source*: Experience Matters.)

THE VALUE AND VULNERABILITY OF INFORMATION ASSETS

Of all the intangible assets, Information Assets are arguably the most valuable. Without data, information and knowledge, no business activity can be undertaken, no business process can be conducted, and no business decision can be made. The Leader's Data Manifesto[6] asserts that "Your organisation's best opportunities for organic growth lie in data". This assertion is corroborated in Chapter 5.

As discussed in Chapter 1 data, information and knowledge can only be regarded as valuable assets and of benefit if the assets can be found and used. If Information Assets can't be found and used, their potential benefit becomes negative, and they very quickly move from being assets to being liabilities. The business impact of how Information Assets are managed, including the extraordinary costs of Information Liabilities is explored in Chapter 5.

What is the value to an organisation of an outstanding Chair or Chief Executive Officer (CEO)? What is the value of that person's knowledge, wisdom and judgement? What is the risk to the organisation of that person leaving or, worse, suffering a career-ending catastrophe? In the height of the pandemic, what would have been the value to a council, county, state or country of knowing where every single COVID-19 case was? What is the value to an organisation of its Information Assets and the benefit of managing them well? This topic will also be explored in Chapter 5.

Information Assets can also be extremely vulnerable. The issue of security and access is one of the most important for Information Asset Managers. How do you ensure that you are providing access to the right information by the right people?

INFORMATION ASSET GOVERNANCE AND MANAGEMENT

In Chapter 1 we defined governance as "who makes what decisions to ensure effective management". Governance is about oversight and controls. Management involves "making and implementing the decisions". Management is about driving business value through execution.

Information Asset governance is defined by DAMA as "The exercise of authority and control (planning, monitoring and enforcement) over the management of Information Assets".[7] All organisations make decisions about data, information and knowledge regardless of whether or not they have a formal Information Asset governance function. Those that establish a formal governance programme exercise authority and control with greater intention.[8] Such organisations are better able to increase the value they get from their Information Assets.[9]

Information Asset governance:

- imposes accountability for the quality of Information Assets; and
- provides a strategic framework for the:
  o control of Information Assets,
  o measurement of the quality of Information Assets, and
  o creation of a culture of recognising Information Asset:
    ▪ value,
    ▪ benefit, and
    ▪ management.

The term "Information Asset Management" (IAM) refers to the processes and procedures used to deploy Information Assets to derive meaningful business insights and deliver those insights to consumers at the right time in the right format.[10] It guides how Information Assets are managed throughout their lifecycle. It identifies what information is important to meeting the organisation's objectives. It ensures that data, information and knowledge are treated as assets in the true business sense and avoids the risk and cost associated with misuse of data and content or exposure to regulatory scrutiny. Everyone in an organisation, especially executives, should therefore understand the importance of effective Information Asset management to their organisation. The management of Information Assets is everyone's job.

In her introduction to the DMBoK, Laura Sebastian-Coleman says,

> Many organisations recognise that their data is a vital enterprise asset. Data and information can give them insight about their customers, products, and services. It can help them innovate and reach strategic goals. Despite that recognition, few organisations actively manage data as an asset from which they can derive ongoing value.

(Evans and Price 2012)

IS THIS NEW?

Is managing data, information and knowledge new? No, it's not. Language, stories and wisdom have been passed down from generation to generation for tens of thousands of years. For example:

We have evidence that the first Australians, the indigenous peoples, have been living on the continent for at least 50,000 years. Over 250 peoples, each with their own distinct languages, call Australia home. A few years ago, I was sitting with some mates around a campfire on the lands of the Pitjantjatjara people. An old bloke called Peter, a Traditional Owner and Custodian of the Pitjantjatjara lands came up to us and said, "I'm going to teach you whitefellas a bit about my culture." Indigenous Australian culture is an oral culture, not written. History, laws, food and water sources, indeed everything that is required for the survival of a society, are captured and promulgated in song. It is called the "Songlines" or the "Dreamtime". Peter began singing in ancient Pitjantjatjara. His words are now disused, but are still intelligible, like our words "thee" and "thine" and "vouchsafe." He sang about The Snowman. The last time there was snow in the Pitjantjatjara lands was in the last Ice Age, 11,000 years ago. His song has been handed down, word for word, from generation to generation for eleven millennia. That is reliable Information Asset management!

Charles Babbage, an English mathematician, philosopher, inventor and mechanical engineer, originated the concept of a digital programmable computer. In 1864, Babbage was reported as saying,

> The whole of the developments and operations of analysis are now capable of being executed by machinery. ... As soon as an Analytical Engine exists, it will necessarily guide the future course of science.[11]

In 1942 at Bletchley Park, Alan Turing and his team built a machine to break the Germans' Enigma codes and provide vital intelligence to the Allies. The information gained from the machine is estimated to have shortened the Second World War by at least two years, saving at least 14 million lives.

In the 1980s, the fifth floor of the Australian headquarters of a global IT vendor was filled with typists working on word processors. Tea ladies pushed their trolleys around the building serving morning and afternoon drinks. They were the consummate Knowledge Managers for they knew everything that was going on. The company had receptionists and secretaries and filing clerks. Documents were held in triplicate. And people could find anything. We could find everything.

The point is that we have lost control over managing our data, information and knowledge well.

WHAT GOOD AND BAD INFORMATION ASSET MANAGEMENT LOOKS LIKE

Throughout this book we will describe and, in tables summarise, what good and bad look like.

"What good Information Asset management looks like" is based on a branch of the Australian Defence Forces. This is an organisation that provides industry oversight and assurance. The organisation has every chance of creating a world's best Information Asset management environment with the privately stated intent of reducing the expenditure of hundreds of billions of dollars by one-third. Other benefits will include creating Australian sovereign capability, reducing the time taken to create that capability and deploy it in the field, and improving the ability of the country to defend itself. Nice.

The Executive Director (ED), in other terms the CEO, runs the organisation in an inverted manner. Unlike traditional management models, in which decision-making is abdicated upwards towards the apex of the organisation, decision-making is delegated down to the lowest possible level. Every person in the organisation understands their job, what the organisation expects of them, what success looks like, how they will be measured and how they will be rewarded. People do what they are paid to do and, to maximise their remuneration, staff find proactive and creative ways to work as efficiently and as effectively as possible. Naturally, both staff and management want to know where they are on the path to meeting their objectives.

That demands high-quality information, firstly for measurement and reward. Secondly, poor Information Asset management creates inefficiencies and waste that prevents staff from reaching their professional goals.

When it comes to the governance and management of the organisation's Information Assets, we asked the Executive Director,

Would you accept accountability for the management of the organisation's data, information and knowledge?

Why would I do that?

Because the management of Information Assets is a business issue that requires corporate discipline, and you are the [only] person in this organisation with the raw authority to impose standards and behaviours on every part of the business.

The ED accepted. When I told Laura Sebastian-Coleman that story, she pushed her chair away for her desk, and she bowed. Wow.

"What bad Information Asset management looks like" is based on an Australian State Government agency. This is an organisation that thinks it can create:

- "a high-performing organisation of excellence"; with
- "an innovative, agile and collaborative workforce"; that
- "delivers effective and efficient public services"; to
- "its key clients, including [the agency's] employees, the [agency's] executive, [its] ministers and central government agencies",

by installing a finance software package, a human resources package and an electronic documents and records management system in the absence of executive interest or involvement. The initiative became three IT projects with no business engagement. It would be serious if it wasn't so risible, but then, who cares? It's only taxpayers' money. The following is a summary of what good and bad Information Asset management looks like:

What good looks like	• **Focus**: The organisation is focused on driving improvement, outcomes and benefits for all stakeholders.
	• **Understanding of Value**: The cost, value and benefits of Information Assets are understood, measured, formally recognised and regularly reported on to the most senior level of the organisation. This infers that a justification model that allows the recognition of intangible assets, risk mitigation and non-financial benefits is in place.
	• **Continuous Improvement**: Investment is made in data quality on a continuous improvement basis.
	• **Accountability**: A senior executive is truly accountable, and has authority, for good Information Asset management. Information Asset management is the responsibility of the business.
	• **Good Behaviour** is encouraged, and bad behaviour is discouraged through corporate discipline, KPIs, measurement and incentives. Data Quality, good decision-making, stakeholder communication, an understanding of What's In It For Me (WIIFM), i.e. targeted benefits, and staff professionalism and satisfaction are high.
	• **Strategic Perspective**: A culture of valuing data, information and knowledge as a vital and strategic business asset is sustained through, and despite, organisation and executive changes.

What bad looks like	• **Lack of Focus**: The organisation is moribund with stifling bureaucracy suffocating change and preventing business improvement. The organisation is risk and process rather than outcomes focussed. Management is more interested in its own welfare than that of the organisation's clients and its other stakeholders.
	• **Unclear/Unknown Value**: The executive has no understanding of the cost, value and benefit of Information Assets. Lazy accounting ensures that only cost reductions are recognised as a benefit.
	• **No Concept of Improvement**: Information is managed by low paid Information/ Records Managers who have job descriptions that include, "answering telephones, filling photocopiers with paper and removing staples."
	• **Bad Behaviour**: Information Management is treated as a cost centre the expenditure on which is to be minimised rather than a source of business benefit to be maximised.
	• **Investment** is justified based on capital expenditure on computing software and hardware projects. The IT Department is made responsible for the management of Information Assets.
	• **No Executive Accountability**: Nobody is held accountable and consequently management has no interest in enforcing Information Asset principles, policy and standards. Stakeholder engagement and good communication are discouraged. Inefficiency, mistakes and bad decisions, heightened business risk, poor quality work and staff dissatisfaction are rife.

HOW INFORMATION ASSETS ARE MANAGED

In Chapter 1 we explained how money is managed. Money has a framework that provides a financial single source of truth. It is diligently reported on. It has carefully delegated authority and responsibility and it has true accountability. We noted that the same is true for Human and Physical Assets. However, the same is not true for Information Assets.

We also mentioned in Chapter 1 that the International Financial Reporting Standard and the US's Generally Accepted Accounting Principles do not allow for the capitalising of Information Assets and including them on the balance sheet, making accounting for them difficult.

Curiously, as we noted in the preface, some boards and executives pay scant attention to the management of the organisation's Information Assets because there is no associated crisis; there is no catalyst for action. They seem to be like a 'corporate Red Adair', looking for the latest thing to blow up so they can fix it. We prefer to think that a little preventative action, quiet professionalism and pursuit of excellence go a long way.

We have asserted that of the assets and resources available to the organisation, its intangible assets are the most valuable and contribute 90% of the S&P 500's market value. And of our intangible assets, our Information Assets are the most valuable.

Yet, typically organisations fail to effectively govern and manage their most valuable assets. They do not know precisely what our organisations do, what Information Assets are used in the production process, the value and vulnerability of those assets, or who uses those assets for what purpose. They do not know what a Business Classification Scheme (an Information Chart of Accounts) is, let alone its profound and strategic value. They do not think that there should be a single place for every Information Asset and every Information Asset should be in its place. They don't know what instruments, like metadata and security models, they need to manage their Information Assets. They hold nobody accountable; there are very few, if any, CIOs who will be sacked if information is not provided to the people who need it in a timely and accurate manner. They do not manage or measure data quality. They do not provide incentives for good Information Asset management behaviour. They do not continually invest in improving data quality and they do not measure or recognise the benefits of doing so. They do not manage their Information Assets with discipline and rigour.

So, if you are not managing your data, information and knowledge with the same level of accountability, discipline and rigour as that with which you manage our financial assets and other resources, it's time you did.

Let's go further; let's look at this logically. If:

1. business performance is driven by how efficiently and effectively the organisation's productive resources are deployed;
2. the job of management is to deploy the organisation's scarce and valuable resources;
3. the most valuable of the organisation's deployable assets available to management are its Intangible Assets;
4. the most valuable of the organisation's Intangible Assets are its Information Assets; and
5. either actively or passively the organisation's executive decides to manage its Information Assets sub-optimally; then

deciding to manage the organisation's most valuable assets sub-optimally is the equivalent of deciding to manage the organisation badly is negligence.

Continuing the story about the global IT vendor, in 1987 personal computers were rolled out to the entire organisation. We justified it on the basis of cost reduction. What cost reduction? The reduction in the salary costs of the typists, tea ladies, receptionists, secretaries and filing clerks. Did the work they did go away? No. So, who did it? Everyone did it. Without a single word of policy, training or instruction. At that moment we lost control of our most important asset – our information. And we have never recovered. This story has been repeated countless times around the world.

Boards and executives typically think that managing Information Assets is a necessary cost rather than an opportunity to leveraged and maximised. They abdicate their governance duties and delegate responsibility to Records Managers and the Information Technology Department who have neither the authority nor the incentives to manage those assets well. As an example, tasks in the job descriptions of the information management team of a large South Australian government agency included "answering telephones, filling photocopiers with paper and removing staples", not exactly high-value work.

The resource-based approach mentioned in Chapter 1 suggests that information should not be treated as an overhead expense, but as a source of business benefit Although they are hard to account for, these assets have significant potential benefits and "just because intangibles cannot be counted on the balance sheet does not mean that they do not count and should not be counted".[12] This approach to focus on business benefit is particularly suitable for application to the enterprise information resources of organisations where the cost of information is often high and where there is a growing need to justify such costs by positioning information as a strategic and important business asset.[13]

WHAT YOUR MATES ARE SAYING

In Chapter 3 we explain the research into the "Barriers to the effective deployment of Information Assets". In this research into what gets in the way of good information asset management, we talked to senior executives on three continents. They told similar stories of limited understanding and missed opportunity. Our interviewees were exclusively senior executives. The following are some of their comments:

The Chief Executive Officer of a process manufacturing company said, "We haven't appointed somebody in a chief information or chief knowledge officer position, because of cost [...]. It's a pretty rudimentary view, a very tactical view, given the apparent value I've placed on information. It"s something we should do. How do I make an excuse for not doing that; it doesn't seem sensible does it?"

When asked if she would participate in our Information Asset management research project the Chair of the Board of a financial institution, which is effectively an information management organisation with a banking licence said, "To be honest, I don't really know much about this area and therefore don't really think I can assist you."

The Managing Director of a law firm observed, "Information Assets are less tangible than the organisation's financial assets and therefore they are not respected in the same way and are managed more haphazardly."

An Equity Partner of a law firm noted, "We have plenty of data all over the place, but because they are not connected it is a total failure."

Another Partner of a law firm said, "Performance management does not include a focus on information management and there are no consequences for negative or inappropriate behaviour. Information management is not on the checklist of our partner reviews."

Yet another Partner said, "Information is not managed with the same rigour as financial assets (money), it is like chalk and cheese."

The Chair of the Board of a financial advisory firm asserted, "The quality of information and how it is stored, maintained and managed is a long way behind that of finances and other assets. The management of the finances is on tertiary school level, while our information management practices are on primary school level."

The Data Manager of a bank lamented, "We spent a lot of time fixing holes in the bucket and beating it into different shapes. But, fundamentally the stuff inside was still rancid. What was in there wasn't right and we needed to get it fixed. So, the approach we've taken for many years is that we would put chemicals in the bucket to try and purify the water. Well, somebody else comes along and throws more rubbish into it and makes it polluted again, because we haven't really looked at what the problem is, what is actually causing that pollution of the water in the bucket."

An Australian financial institution appointed a Chief Data Officer (CDO). Everybody was excited. But, as she was four levels below the Chief Executive Officer, she was a Chief Nothing, she couldn't influence data management behaviours and the executive had set her up for failure.

In 2017 a Victorian State government department advertised a job for "anyone interested in an exciting role with the Victorian Electoral Commission … Records Management Administrator". The job description included, "Administrative assistance, including maintaining and arranging postal credit, stock maintenance and service requirements associated with franking machine and special mail items, Reception relief, catering, ordering milk".

It appears from these quotations and examples that management has little apparent interest in managing the Information Assets of their organisations well and, presumably, the performance of their organisations.

Earlier we asserted that "data, information and knowledge are only valuable assets and of benefit if they can be found and used". To find and use Information Assets is very simple; you just need to know what it's been called and where it's been put.

And herein lies the problem.

There is no software in the world that can work properly without the right data. If you put rubbish data into a system, the results you get out cannot be anything but rubbish.

The concept of "garbage in, garbage out" has been around for a very long time. In 1864, Charles Babbage, to whom we have referred above, said,

> On two occasions I have been asked [by members of Parliament], "Pray, Mr Babbage, if you put into the machine wrong figures, will the right answers come out?" I am not able rightly to apprehend the kind of confusion of ideas that could provoke such a question.[14]

Brilliant. On 10 November 1957, a US Army Specialist named William D. Mellin explained that

> if the problem has been sloppily programmed the answer will be just as incorrect. If the programmer made mistakes the machine will make mistakes. It can't correct them because it can't do one thing. It can't think for itself.

You can spend millions on technology, but it's pointless if the quality of the organisation's Information Assets is poor. The CEO of a large US health organisation said, "I have invested in technology to the point where I can receive crap at the speed of light". So why aren't we paying attention to the quality of our data, information and knowledge?

Further, there is no software in the world that can get the right data for itself. No software can run around the organisation and determine for itself what the organisation does, the assets it deploys, who does what, the data, information and knowledge they use every day, the value and vulnerability of those Information Assets to whom, where to put them and what to call them, and when to destroy them, so the right information is made available to the right people at the right time.

Artificial Intelligence and products like ChatGPT, which was released in November 2022, are currently taking the world by storm. However, ChatGPT can only help you find information, it can't help you manage it.

The risk, cost, value, benefit and ethics associated with Information Assets are contextual. Context requires judgement. Judgement is human. Software alone cannot do the job; it requires business knowledge and good corporate behaviour. Good corporate behaviour requires understanding, order and discipline. Organisations must treat their Information Assets the way they treat their money – with frameworks, tools, responsibility and accountability.

At some stage somebody has to instil the corporate discipline that ensures that the organisation's critical Information Assets are readily available to the goodies and protected from the baddies. This is not a cyber issue, although cyber has a bit part to play; this is an Information Asset management issue. If the organisation manages its Information Assets well, then compliance, security and other risk mitigation measures drop out of the bottom. Buying software does not absolve you of your governance and management responsibilities.

Our research shows that management:
- abdicates its responsibility to manage its organisation's information as a business asset;
- confuses managing its Information Assets with managing the technology that delivers them;
- defaults the responsibility of managing information to IT, rather than delegating it to the business where it belongs;
- believes vendors telling them that just installing software will address its information management problems.

Management needs to stop looking for a
silver Information Technology bullet.
Instead, management needs to bite the bullet
and manage its Information Assets with the
same discipline and rigour as that with
which it manages its Financial Assets.

(*Source:* Experience Matters)

- What Information Assets does your organisation have and deploy? Is corporate knowledge treated as an asset?
- Of these, which are the most valuable? How is the value calculated?
- Which are the most vulnerable? How is the vulnerability identified?
- Of the contribution made to the organisation by Intangible Assets, how much is made by your Information Assets? How is that contribution calculated?
- What would your organisation be worth without any data, information or knowledge?
- When does an Information Asset become an Information Liability?
- Which of your data, information and knowledge are Information Assets and which are Information Liabilities? Why would you hang onto Information Liabilities?
- What could be the cost to your organisation of its Information Liabilities?
- How are Information Assets, including that data, information and knowledge that is no longer of value to the organisation, managed throughout their lifecycle?

NOTES

1. Evans, N. & Price, J. 2014. Responsibility and Accountability for Information Asset Management (IAM) in Organisations. *Electronic Journal of Information Systems and Evaluation (EJISE)*, 17(1): 113–121.

2. Baida, Z. 2020. Data, the Most Valuable Resource. *Insights Unboxed*. Available at: https://insightsunboxed.com/data-the-most-valuable-resource-ziv-baida/

3. Redman, T. 2008. *Data Driven*. Harvard Business Press.

4. Shannon, C. E. 1948. A Mathematical Theory of Communication. *Bell System Technical Journal,* July: 379–423.

5. All currency is Australian dollars unless otherwise stated.

6. https://dataleaders.org/manifesto/.

7. Knight, M. 2021. What Is Data Governance? *Dataversity*. Available at: https://www.dataversity.net/what-is-data-governance/.

8. Seiner, R. (2014). *Non-Invasive Data Governance: The Path of Least Resistance and Greatest Success*. Technics Publications, LLC

9. DAMA International. 2017. *DAMA-DMBOK: Data Management Body of Knowledge* (2nd Edition). Technics Publications, LLC.

10. Bhatt, Y., & Thirunavukkarasu, A. (2010). Information Management: A Key for Creating Business Value. *The Data Administration Newsletter*. Available at http://www.tdan.com/view-articles/12829.

11. Babbage, C. (1864). *Passages from the Life of a Philosopher*. Longman, Roberts and Green: London.

12. Higson, C., & Waltho, D. (2009) Valuing Information as an Asset. *SAS the Power to Know*, 1–17. Available at: http://faculty.london.edu/chigson/research/InformationAsset.pdf.

13. Evans, N., & Price, J. (2020). Development of a Holistic Model for the Management of an Enterprise's Information Assets. *International Journal of Information Management*, 54.

14. Babbage, C. (1864). *Passages from the Life of a Philosopher*. Longman, Roberts and Green: London.

3

What Is Preventing You from Governing and Managing Your Information Assets Well?

INTRODUCTION

In Chapter 2 we:

1. defined and described Information Assets;
2. discovered the value and vulnerability of Information Assets;
3. showed how Information Assets are managed; and
4. differentiated between Information Assets and Information Technology.

In this chapter we will:

1. describe our research into the barriers to managing Information Assets well;
2. present the findings of the investigation;
3. explain each of the identified barriers; and
4. identify the root causes of ineffective information management to be addressed.

We have argued that understanding what the organisation does and how it does it is critical to deciding what resources are required for every business activity, every business process and every business decision. We have further proposed that Information Assets are the lifeblood of an organisation but are rarely managed well. In this chapter we identify the barriers to governing and managing those vital business assets. This gives you the chance to address

DOI: 10.4324/9781003439141-3

those barriers. It's like when you have a wasp in the room – you want to be able to see it.

EXECUTIVE OVERVIEW

In this chapter we describe our approach to conducting pragmatic, rigorous and academically sound research to identify the "barriers to effective deployment of Information Assets", the business impact of existing information management practices, the measures available to organisations to improve their Information Asset management and the benefits to organisations from doing so. We conducted personal interviews with more than 70 CxO level executives to identify how leaders think about the management of their organisations' Information Assets – and the risk, cost, value, benefit and ethics associated with those assets. The findings identified:

- limited executive awareness and understanding about the importance of Information Assets to their organisations;
- an inability to justify investment in managing Information Assets well;
- a lack of governance at both business and asset levels;
- inadequate leadership in and management of Information Assets; and
- limitations in the enabling systems and practices.[1]

THE CATALYST FOR OUR RESEARCH

An organisation's Information Assets are key contributors to its capacity to deliver its products and services in the most efficient and effective manner. Every organisation we have studied recognises that it has data, information and knowledge that is of value to it. Ocean Tomo's work suggests that Intangible Assets now contribute 90% of the market value of the S&P500 and Experience Matters' industry knowledge indicates that the potential tangible benefits from improving the management of Information Assets are conservatively estimated at $20,000 per knowledge worker per year. This is explained in Chapter 6. Management in both government and corporate sectors is becoming aware of the critical importance of these assets being well understood, being properly managed and playing a pivotal role in the strategic management process. It is accepted that the effective management of Information Assets is increasingly critical to organisations' success.

The evidence is compelling. Stuart Hamilton wrote,

> I have been reading the "Barriers to the Effective Deployment of Information Assets." Thanks for that. It is one of those things that you see every day, but you don't see it because it is so much like bland wallpaper that covers everything. Once it is explained, so that you can see it as a business pathology, it resonates in many ways.
>
> Even in our case we are in the information management business, and we have very deep investments in the most up to date information technologies and in data collection. However, for lack of management of information as a strategic asset we make marketing decisions and deploy sales resources without tightly focused information about our target markets. We make design and development decisions without accurate information about end-use requirements and market demand.
>
> We have lots of data, but we don't have a coordinated data collection strategy, so we have no way of knowing how representative our data are with respect to our information requirements. Every decision-maker tries to assemble meaningful information from whatever data is opportunistically available, but we don't have a coordinated and efficient information management strategy.
>
> We need to ask the question: "Who needs what information, for what purpose, and how are they going to get it?", and the corollary: "How much would information management as a strategic investment cost and what would be the sum of benefits?"
>
> We are very smart people with a deep commitment to data-driven decisions. What we have been missing is an understanding of a few key concepts. Evans and Price (2012) should be compulsory reading for every executive and business entrepreneur... I do believe that you have documented the greatest single barrier to productivity in the 21st Century economy and nobody knows about it.

However, as we saw in Chapter 2, anecdotal and research evidence indicates that organisations govern and manage their information and knowledge on a best effort basis as an administrative overhead to be minimised with predictable, suboptimal results, rather than on a strategic basis as a critical business enabler, to be invested in, leveraged and exploited to mitigate business risk and drive business benefit. Every organisation we have studied

TABLE 3.1

How Well Are Information Assets Managed?

We have substantial anecdotal and research evidence that managing Information Assets well helps:	We have substantial anecdotal evidence that executives just don't care. They:
• mitigate business risk; • protect corporate and individual reputations; • improve competitive advantage; • improve product and service provision; • drive operational and financial benefits; and • increase staff professionalism and morale.	• don't know about Information Assets; • aren't asked about Information Assets; • don't know how to manage Information Assets; • can't cost or value or measure the benefits from managing Information Assets; and • have other priorities.

acknowledges that its Information Assets are not managed as well as they could or should be (Table 3.1).

The discrepancy between the value and benefit associated with Information Assets and the lack of their governance and management clearly constitutes a business contradiction – a business contradiction that we are researching.

Yet, the situation is perceived to be neither a problem nor an opportunity. We need empirical evidence of how managing Information Assets affects business risk and performance, and we need global academic, media and business recognition of the problem.

The fundamental question is why? This question constitutes the basis of our work, the purpose of which is to conduct pragmatic, rigorous and academically sound research to determine the "barriers to effective deployment of Information Assets", the business impact of existing information management practices, the measures available to organisations to improve their Information Asset management and the benefits to organisations from doing so. We are identifying how leaders think about the management of their organisations' Information Assets – and the risk, cost, value, benefit and ethics associated with those assets.

HOW WE CONDUCTED OUR RESEARCH

The overall objective of our research is to ignite global recognition that the management of Information Assets:

- is important to organisations;
- is able to be improved; and
- can deliver significant business outcomes.

In designing our research project, we followed three principles:

1. **uniqueness** – it has to be pioneering;
2. **relevance** – it has to pass the "so what" test; and
3. **integrity** – it has to be above reproach.

With reference to these principles:

1. we conducted our own unique research to validate or disprove our thinking and the anecdotes from experience. But, what we have been doing is true research; it's like the USS Enterprise, "going where no man has gone before";
2. the project passes the "so what" test. Organisations that have embraced our findings have been highly successful in their Information Asset management projects. As mentioned in Chapter 1, Greg Pearce said, "There is no other project in our entire investment portfolio that could have delivered a greater result, more quickly, with better staff satisfaction"; and
3. the project is ethics approved and peer reviewed, putting it above academic reproach.

We are pretty pleased with the feedback we have been receiving for our research. In addition to the kind words of Stuart Hamilton and Laura Sebastian-Coleman:

- Doug Laney declared, "your work is tremendous…your research is ground-breaking".
- Mike Orzen, Principal of Mike Orzen & Associates, winner of the Shingo Prize for Operational Excellence wrote, "We consider [Experience Matters'] to be great work of the utmost importance … The research findings are… testament to their global thought leadership and practice … you are doing great work".

Amongst many others, Board members and C-Level executives of organisations that include Australian Rail Track Corporation, Bell Helicopter

(USA), Boeing (USA), City of Cape Town (South Africa), ConWay (USA), EDS (USA), Glacier (South Africa), Hewlett Packard (USA), Lowes (USA), National Australia Bank, Sanlam (South Africa), Verizon Communications (USA), and Wells Fargo (USA) have all participated.

A list of interviewees is presented in Table 3.2.

WHAT OUR RESEARCH FOUND

Following our consultation, we added the hundreds of research findings and quotations, to our years of project anecdotes and observations. We then categorised the plethora of findings, anecdotes and quotations. To categorise them we conducted a root cause analysis on the findings. We asked, "why" until we could ask "why" no more. The ultimate reason for poor Information Asset practices is "bad management". It is a useless finding; it is not sufficiently granular and you can't do anything with it. So, we regressed to "bad management minus one". At "bad management minus one" the findings fell out into the five categories of barrier, namely:

1. a lack of executive **awareness and understanding** about the importance of Information Assets to their organisations;
2. a lack of a **justification** model and an inability to justify investment in managing Information Assets well;
3. a lack of **governance** at both business and asset levels;
4. a lack of **leadership in and management** of Information Assets; and
5. a catch-all category of **enabling systems and practices**.

Finding 1: Awareness and Understanding

Barriers under the category of awareness and understanding identified by the executives we interviewed include the following:

- the problem is not recognised. Organisations do not realise the risk of not managing their Information Assets effectively;
- there is very little formal training in the management of Information Assets. There is a lack of formal, particularly tertiary, postgraduate and executive, education; and little on the job education;

TABLE 3.2

Research Participants

INTERVIEWEE	ROLE	INDUSTRY	LOCATION
1.	Data Management	Finance	Melbourne
2.	MD	Recruitment	Adelaide
3.	Managing Partner	Legal	Adelaide
4.	Board	Finance	Adelaide
5.	CFO	Finance	Adelaide
6.	CFO	Utilities – Rail	Adelaide
7.	CKO	Utilities – Gas	Adelaide
8.	CKO	Government – State	Adelaide
9.	CFO	Finance	Adelaide
10.	CEO	Manufacturing	Adelaide
11.	CFO	Services - Member	Adelaide
12.	CFO	Resources	Adelaide
13.	CFO	Finance	Adelaide
14.	CEO	ICT	Cape Town
15.	CIO	Finance - Insurance	Cape Town
16.	CIO	Finance	Cape Town
17.	CIO	Government – Local	Cape Town
18.	CIO	Government – State	Columbia, Maryland
19.	CIO	Government – Local	Columbia, Maryland
20.	CIO	Government – State	Columbia, Maryland
21.	CIO	Hospitality	Columbia, Maryland
22.	Vice President (VP) IT Services	Education – Tertiary	Dallas, Texas
23.	CEO	ICT	Dallas, Texas
24.	Director IT	Manufacturing	Dallas, Texas
25.	CIO	ICT	Dallas, Texas
26.	Fellow	ICT	Dallas, Texas
27.	CIO	ICT	Dallas, Texas
28.	CEO	ICT	Dallas, Texas
29.	Director Integrated Clinical Services	Health	Portland, Oregon
30.	VP Application Development	Transport	Portland, Oregon
31.	Director Management Information Services	Manufacturing	Portland, Oregon

(Continued)

TABLE 3.2 (CONTINUED)

Research Participants

INTERVIEWEE	ROLE	INDUSTRY	LOCATION
32.	IT Director	Retail	Mooresville, North Carolina
33.	Senior Vice President	Finance	Charlotte, North Carolina
34.	Vice President IT	Manufacturing	Fort Mill, South Carolina
35.	Marketing and Brand Strategist	Hospitality	Chicago, Illinois
36.	Principal	Finance	Chicago, Illinois
37.	Media Director and Strategist	Marketing	Chicago, Illinois
38.	Software Executive	ICT	Chicago, Illinois
39.	Sales and Marketing	ICT	Chicago, Illinois
40.	Director Data Governance	Health	Chicago, Illinois
41.	Principal	Finance	Chicago, Illinois
42.	Senior Director	Finance	Chicago, Illinois
43.	Client Director	Advisory	Chicago, Illinois
44.	Owner	Legal	Pretoria
45.	Managing Director	Legal	Pretoria
46.	Director	Legal	Pretoria
47.	Chairman of the Board	Legal	Pretoria
48.	Director	Legal	Pretoria
49.	Lawyer	Legal	Johannesburg
50.	Partner, Knowledge Management	Legal	Johannesburg
51.	Partner	Legal	Pretoria
52.	Chair	Insurance, Defence	Adelaide
53.	Chair	Utilities	Adelaide
54.	Chair	Community Care	Adelaide
55.	Chair	Finance	Adelaide
56.	CIO	Legal	Adelaide
57.	CIO	Defence	Adelaide
58.	CIO	Insurance	Adelaide
59.	CIO	Health	Adelaide

(*Continued*)

TABLE 3.2 (CONTINUED)

Research Participants

INTERVIEWEE	ROLE	INDUSTRY	LOCATION
60.	Director Learning and Business Knowledge	Government	Adelaide
61.	CIO	Education	Adelaide
62.	Managing Partner	Legal	Adelaide
63.	Director	Legal	Adelaide
64.	Chief Operating Officer	Legal	Melbourne
65.	Chief Operating Officer	Legal	Adelaide
66.	Chief Information Officer	Legal	Adelaide
67.	Director, IT and Cyber Security	Government	Montgomery County, Maryland
68.	Attorney	Legal	Washington DC
69.	COO	Legal	Washington DC
70.	Named Equity Partner	Legal	Gaithersburg, Maryland
71.	Data Management Lead	Legal in Government	Montgomery County, Maryland
72.	Lawyer	Legal	Sydney

- retention of knowledge becomes an important challenge; and
- people retiring or leaving the organisation take their information with them.

We explore the topic of executive awareness in more detail in Chapter 6.

Finding 2: Justification

Barriers under the category of justification identified by the executives we interviewed are the most numerous and the hardest to address. This is a frustrating and vexatious topic. Barriers include the following:

- there is no catalyst or incentive to manage Information Assets well;
- poor management of Information Assets rarely causes an overt problem;
- certain types of businesses do not warrant action. In certain service industries it pays to be inefficient;

- managing Information Assets gets lost in the day-to-day activities. This is especially true for organisations that are growing rapidly;
- there are burning issues that need to be tended to in the first instance and the management of Information Assets becomes a lower priority;
- external pressure such as a volatile economic climate also impacts on the Information Asset management of businesses;
- it often takes a crisis or severe financial loss to change the organisation's attitude to managing Information Assets;
- compliance requirements are often the only driver;
- the cost of managing Information Assets is unknown and not recorded as accounting standards do not allow organisations to determine these costs, or the costs are too difficult to determine;
- the value of Information Assets and their management is unknown;
- the value of data, information and knowledge is temporally, managerially, and professionally contextual;
- the accounting system doesn't allow a business to value information and record it on the balance sheet;
- the benefits of effective management of Information Assets are unknown;
- the benefits of managing Information Assets well are intangible;
- information is intangible and measuring the benefits of tangible assets is easier;
- benefits of good Information Asset management are intertwined;
- benefits of good Information Asset management are difficult to crystallise. If good Information Asset management improves productivity, how do you sack a percentage of a person;
- management teams usually want to know what the return in hard cash will be on what they will be spending. This is often impossible, as knowledge is an intangible asset;
- data, information and knowledge contribute value to the business as triggers of business processes. It is difficult to value the information itself;
- managing Information Assets is boring;
- people have their own agendas; and
- risk management is seen as a burden.

We explore the topic of justification in more detail in Chapter 14.

Finding 3: Governance

Whilst the topic of justification attracted the most comments from executives throughout the interview process, our anecdotal evidence proves that paying attention to governance, particularly at business level, creates the greatest chances of success. A Board member observed that "From a director's perspective data, information, and knowledge are invisible unless something goes wrong: It's not on the radar. It's not considered to be a big enough risk. It's just not on the agenda. It is difficult to educate boards, and unless the management team elevated the management of information to the board level, it will probably not be done". We will come back to the board members in Chapter 7.

The topics of business and asset governance are addressed in more detail in Chapters 7 and 9, respectively.

Finding 4: Leadership and Management

Barriers under the category of leadership and management identified by the executives we interviewed include the following:

- executive support for managing Information Assets well is absent;
- mistakes are not tolerated which kills the appetite to conduct difficult, nebulous, enterprise-wide initiatives like managing Information Assets well;
- managers who know the organisation well understand how to navigate and get around the vagaries of the information systems;
- there are no rewards and recognition for managing Information Assets well;
- whilst many organisations have an IT or digital transformation strategy, they lack an Information Asset Management vision. Managers focus on information technology, not information management;
- organisations lack discipline in managing information as an enterprise asset. As such, data and information are stored everywhere on people's hard drives and in legacy systems, electronically, in hard copy, in different physical places and accessed by different computers;
- information is isolated and can be neither found and used nor shared;
- there is resistance to change;
- many employees and managers do not value information and there is a lack of perceived benefit of managing it well;

- people often work for their own personal advantage rather than the good of the organisation; and
- finally, and possibly most importantly, employees only take an interest in what is measured and rewarded.

The topic of leadership and management is discussed in more detail in Chapter 8.

Finding 5: Enabling Systems and Practices

Barriers under the category of Enabling Systems and Practices identified by the executives we interviewed include the following:

- business language is imprecise. As we observed in Chapter 1, a university has four different definitions for the term "student commencement". How can you run an organisation like that;
- in Chapter 14 we will discuss how accounting practices do not account for Information Assets;
- the information technology infrastructure has shortcomings. Further detail on this can be found in Chapter 10; and
- maintaining high-quality data and information is too difficult, so staff avoid doing it. More on Information Asset management behaviours can be found in Chapter 11.

Our findings identifying the barriers to the effective management of Information Assets are summarised in Figure 3.1.

In summary, our anecdotal and research evidence has found that, with the exception of getting excited about cyber security, organisations typically do not demonstrate:

- an interest in data, information and knowledge management from Board or senior management level;
- understanding of what the organisation has and how they are deployed to conduct its critical business activities;
- actual or even relative valuation of the organisation's Information Assets;
- the costing of the management of the organisation's Information Assets. As an example, every time an email is opened, a drawing is

created, a contract is written or a meeting is held, data, information and knowledge assets are being deployed and cost is being incurred;

- an ability to understand and address the risks and benefits inherent in the management of Information Assets or to ask penetrating and insightful questions; or
- a propensity to view Information Assets management as a cultural issue and to crystallise and recognise the benefits it produces.

VALIDATION OF OUR FINDINGS

Following the publication of our findings, we conducted another exercise to augment the original root cause analysis done by the authors. Experts in data and information governance and management also contributed. They

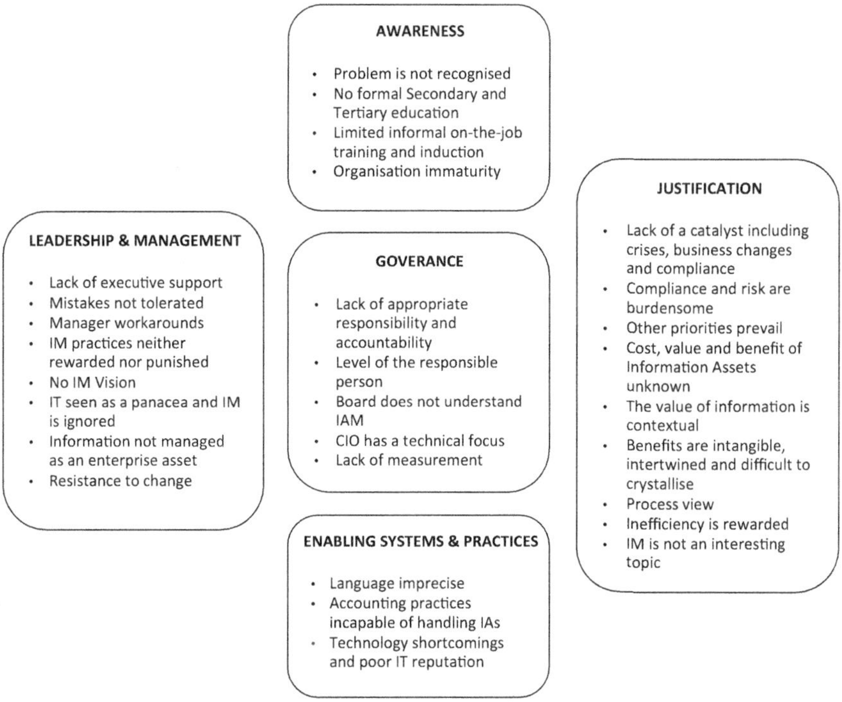

AWARENESS

- Problem is not recognised
- No formal Secondary and Tertiary education
- Limited informal on-the-job training and induction
- Organisation immaturity

JUSTIFICATION

- Lack of a catalyst including crises, business changes and compliance
- Compliance and risk are burdensome
- Other priorities prevail
- Cost, value and benefit of Information Assets unknown
- The value of information is contextual
- Benefits are intangible, intertwined and difficult to crystallise
- Process view
- Inefficiency is rewarded
- IM is not an interesting topic

LEADERSHIP & MANAGEMENT

- Lack of executive support
- Mistakes not tolerated
- Manager workarounds
- IM practices neither rewarded nor punished
- No IM Vision
- IT seen as a panacea and IM is ignored
- Information not managed as an enterprise asset
- Resistance to change

GOVERANCE

- Lack of appropriate responsibility and accountability
- Level of the responsible person
- Board does not understand IAM
- CIO has a technical focus
- Lack of measurement

ENABLING SYSTEMS & PRACTICES

- Language imprecise
- Accounting practices incapable of handling IAs
- Technology shortcomings and poor IT reputation

FIGURE 3.1

Summary of the barriers to the effective management of Information Assets. (*Source*: Authors.)

brought their immense intellect and experience to the exercise and the result is presented as a fishbone diagram in Figure 3.2.

The root cause analysis is a pragmatic tool that organisations can use as a checklist for potential barriers to good Information Asset management. In addition to the root causes documented by the authors, we asked experts to contribute to our findings.

These experts are Danette McGilvray who is the author of "Executing Data Quality Projects – Ten Steps to Quality Data and Trusted Information" and Tom Redman, "the Data Doc", who is the author of "Data Driven" and "Getting in front on data"; Tom regularly publishes in *Harvard Business Review* and *MIT Sloane Management Review*.

Danette's and Tom's additions to the root cause analysis in the fishbone diagram above are explained as follows.

Governance

- Lack of clear management responsibility. Tom Redman[2] points out that

    it is hard to determine who "owns" or is responsible for data on the fly. One could argue that customer service owns the data because it created them. Or one could argue that order fulfillment, inventory management or some other department owns the data because it needs them. Finally, one could argue that IT owns the data because it manages the computers and systems that move the data around. There are obvious strengths and weaknesses to each candidate answer. Unfortunately, in too many organisations the question is simply left unasked.

- Unclear who is responsible for what. Tom goes further by saying,

    Avoiding the "if it's in the computer it must be the province of IT" trap pays enormous dividends. Organisations should adopt the stance that data and information are the province of the business. The various departments are responsible for the quality of the data they create and are responsible for ensuring that their people can find the data they need.

Danette McGilvray[3] concurs with "Responsibility refers to the fact that many people should answer for their part in ensuring high quality data. Data work is done by people who, hopefully, know their roles

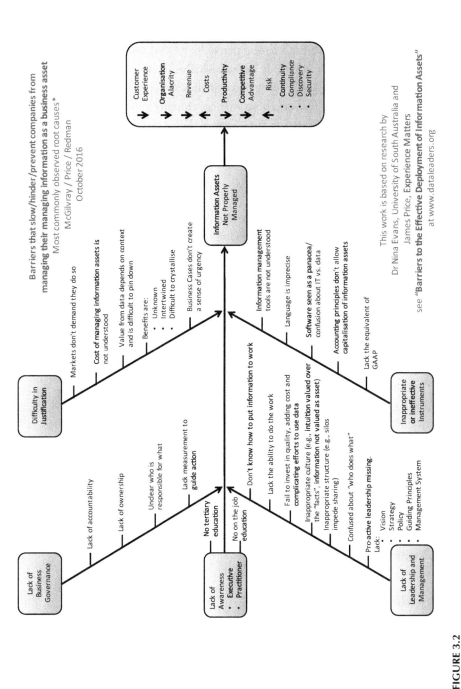

FIGURE 3.2

Barriers to the effective management of Information Assets. (*Source*: Authors.)

and responsibilities". And Laura Sebastian-Coleman points to a 2001 PwC survey that concluded that "IT departments were perceived as responsible for data management issues" and that "responsibility for data management is in the wrong place".[4]

- Lack of measurement to guide action. Measurement provides visibility that should prompt appropriate action based on what is seen from the measures. Very few organisations continually monitor the quality of its Information Assets. It therefore makes it extremely difficult to continually improve Information Asset management practices.

Leadership and Management

- Don't know how to put Information Assets to work – According to Tom Redman many organisations don't know how to put Information Assets to work to:
  o enhance decision-making;
  o improve innovation;
  o build data into their products, services and processes;
  o improve quality, eliminate costs and build trust;
  o establish and maintain a competitive advantage over their competitors by exploiting their proprietary data; and
  o monetise their data.[5]
- Lack the ability to do the work. Organisations have neither the capacity nor the capability in their staff to leverage and capitalise on their Information Assets.
- Inappropriate structure – There is no single source of truth/single system of record and silos of data, information and knowledge impede sharing.
- Proactive leadership missing – There is no key person driving the culture of managing data, information and knowledge as a strategic business asset.

Justification

- Markets don't demand they do so – This is slowly changing, but too slowly. Cyber insurance is emerging, and class actions are being brought against organisations that allow their data to be stolen.

Inappropriate or Ineffective Instruments

* Information Asset management tools are not understood. Instruments like Business Classification Schemes are not understood, let alone their profound strategic value.

NOTES

1. Evans, N., & Price, J. 2012. Barriers to the Effective Deployment of Information Assets: An Executive Management Perspective. *Interdisciplinary Journal of Information and Knowledge Management (IJIKM)*, 7: 177–199.
2. Redman, Thomas C. 2008. *Data Driven*. Harvard Business Press: Brighton, Massachusetts.
3. McGilvray, D. 2021. *Executing Data Quality Projects (2nd edition)*. TM. Morgan Kaufmann Publishers Inc.: San Francisco.
4. Sebastian-Coleman, L. 2022. *Meeting the Challenges of Data Quality Management (1st edition)*. Elsevier Science.
5. Redman, Thomas C. 2008. *Data Driven*. Harvard Business Press: Brighton, Massachusetts.

4

Which Areas Should You Focus on to Manage Your Information Assets Well?: A Holistic Model for Doing So

INTRODUCTION

In Chapter 3 we:

1. described our research into the barriers to governing and managing Information Assets well;
2. presented the findings of the research;
3. explained each of the identified barriers; and
4. identified the root causes of ineffective information management to be addressed.

In this chapter we will:

1. explain maturity models and assessment;
2. discuss the development of the Holistic Information Asset Management Model (HIAMMM) which forms the basis of this book; and
3. explain each of the ten focus areas or domains in the Model.

By using this model, you have a method by which you can identify potential barriers to governing and managing Information Assets, understand the maturity of your Information Asset management practices and determine the business impact of those practices on the organisation.

                    DOI: 10.4324/9781003439141-4

EXECUTIVE OVERVIEW

Our research culminated in a Holistic Information Asset Management Model consisting of ten domains that represent the important areas that need to be investigated to determine the maturity of your Information Asset management practices and develop a roadmap to improve them. The first important aspect of the model refers to the business component, which is of interest to stakeholders concerned about business outcomes. The second important aspect is the information component, which holds potential for both business benefits and various business risks. The ten domains relate to business impact, executive awareness, business environment, leadership and management, information environment, information technology, information asset behaviour, information quality, information asset leverage and justification. Bad outcomes in one domain can usually be traced back through multiple others.[1]

In this chapter we explain how our research findings have been deployed to create our Holistic Information Asset Management Maturity Model. To be clear:

- A maturity model identifies the aspects of an organisation against which maturity can be assessed.
- A maturity assessment instrument is the next level of tool development in which the maturity of these aspects of the organisation can be assessed against a fixed scale.
- A maturity assessment is the activity of doing it. A maturity assessment can:
  - assess the "as is" status;
  - specify the desired "to be" situation;
  - evaluate the maturity of the aspect being assessed i.e. where that aspect of the organisation sits in the gap between "as is" and "to be"; and
  - benchmark the results of the assessment (in ascending order of value) against;
    - peers in the industry,
    - standards,
    - corporate objectives and
    - progress over time.

John Ladley describes an Information Asset management maturity model as

> An Information [Asset Management] Maturity Assessment determines the current state of maturity of an organisation to utilise data and information in an advanced manner. Understand what the organisation does with the content and information it produces. Focus is on impressions and feelings business personnel have on how well the company uses and manages data to its advantage. Besides identifying a current state, this activity provides a baseline for measuring progress toward future Data Governance effectiveness from an objective, qualitative standpoint.[2]

The ten domains of the Holistic Information Asset Management Model represent the important areas that need to be investigated as part of a health check to determine the maturity of the Information Asset management practices and addressed when developing a roadmap to improve them.

The ten domains are as. follows

1. Business impact.
2. Executive awareness.
3. Business environment.
4. Leadership and management.
5. Information environment.
6. Information technology.
7. Information Asset behaviour.
8. Information quality.
9. Information Asset leverage.
10. Justification.

We represent the model as in Figure 4.1.

The analogy of the iceberg is used because two important aspects need to be considered.

1. The first aspect is the business component, which is of interest to stakeholders concerned about business outcomes. This is represented by the visible part of the iceberg above the water line.
2. The second aspect, the information component, holds potential for both business benefits and unseen danger. This aspect is represented by the invisible and deceptively large part of the iceberg that is hidden beneath the waterline.

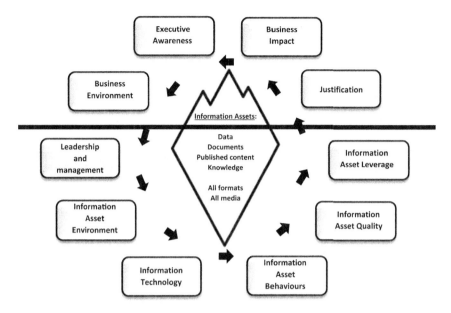

FIGURE 4.1
Holistic Information Asset Management Model. (*Source*: Authors.)

The domains are described as follows.

Domain 1: Business Impact

The business impact domain describes the impact on an organisation of its Information Asset management practices. We start with the business impact, particularly benefits because they are what matters most; no initiative should be undertaken if there is no benefit to the organisation of doing so.

An ability to justify legitimate benefits (Domain 10) means they can be recognised. If the business impact that Information Asset management practices have on the organisation is recognised and understood (Domain 1), executives will take an interest in managing those assets well (Domain 2).

We further explore business impact in Chapter 5.

Domain 2: Executive Awareness

The executive awareness domain assesses the extent to which the Board and Senior Leadership Team are aware of, and advocate the importance of, their Information Assets.

> If the business impact that Information Asset management practices have on the organisation is clearly recognised and understood (Domain 1), executives will take an interest in managing those assets well. If they are aware of, and understand, the importance of their Information Assets and how they are governed and managed (Domain 2), they will impose effective business governance conducive to managing those assets well (Domain 3).

Our research produced a range of observations that indicate a lack of executive awareness as to the importance of Information Assets. Here are some examples.

The CEO of a manufacturing company said, "I have just completed my MBA and I learnt about everything – strategy, risk, governance, finance, IT, HR, the works, but not a word was spoken about the management of information".

A Managing Director observed, "Investors are mostly focused on revenue and costs and therefore managers focus on sales, getting the products to market, collecting and investing the money and making sure it gets onto the books, as well as managing expenses".

We further explore executive awareness in Chapter 6.

Domain 3: Business Environment

The business environment domain addresses the management of the enterprise as a whole – its business governance, its strategy, its business activities and processes, its capability and capacity, its culture and its language. It considers the organisation's business governance that typically addresses "who makes what decisions". This is the level above the organisation's asset governance and management. A lack of business governance is an important reason why organisations are not successful in managing their Information Assets. The

Board rarely imposes effective business governance over the management of the organisation's Information Assets and regards information management as an operational activity, rather than a strategic requirement to mitigate business risk, gain competitive advantage or drive business performance.

> If the Board and Chief Executive Officer are aware of the importance of effective Information Asset management (Domain 2), they will impose effective business governance conducive to managing those assets well (Domain 3). If the organisation is governed well, its leaders and managers will lead by example and create a culture of managing Information Assets well (Domain 4).

A single person is rarely held ultimately accountable for managing data, information and knowledge as a business asset. The Chief Information Officer (CIO) is not the right person to be accountable, as they are usually misnamed and are more properly a Chief Technology Officer. They are measured on IT systems' throughput, uptime, cost and perhaps usability and typically they have a technical focus.[3]

We further explore the business environment in Chapter 7.

Domain 4: Leadership and Management

> With a conducive business environment (Domain 3), the organisation's leaders and managers will lead by example and create a culture of managing Information Assets well (Domain 4). With committed leadership and management (Domain 4), Information Asset management policies and other instruments will be diligently implemented and adherence with them encouraged, creating an effective Information Asset management environment (Domain 5).

The leadership and management domain addresses the organisation's human resources, structure, roles, culture, behaviour and incentives regarding the management of Information Assets.

In Chapter 2 we established that:

1. the management of Information Assets cannot be done by IT; it must be done by the people who understand those assets, i.e. by the business;
2. software alone cannot do the job. The creation of high-quality data must be done by humans; and
3. humans require discipline. You can't call stuff what you like, and put it where you like, without any location information or metadata, and expect it to be easily found and used by the people who need to find and use it. You don't go up to a Chief Financial Officer and say, "What did you do with that million dollars" and have him/her say, "I don't know" as (s)he rummages in cupboards and suitcases and looks under piles of paper. "It must be here somewhere".

Senior management support is crucial for creating a culture of valuing, managing, sharing and leveraging Information Assets. The CEO is often the only executive who is able to take an enterprise view, who cares about the overall performance of the organisation and who is concerned with the creation of sustainable value. (S)he is the only person with the authority and raw power to impose standards and behaviours across the entire organisation. The other executives are typically only interested in what's under their own span of control and they won't countenance a peer or subordinate telling them what to do. With that enterprise view, the CEO needs to galvanise each executive to take a leadership position on the management of Information Assets for their part of the organisation.

The Chief Data Officer of a bank said,

> A challenge we have at the moment, is trying to make sure that at the top they're actually putting the money where their mouth is. It's not because they don't want to or that they don't believe it, there are so many competing priorities.

The Chief Knowledge Officer (CKO) of a government department believes that executives sometimes understand that information and knowledge are valued for purposes of improving the efficiency and effectiveness of the organisation, but he added:

> Would they jump on a sword for that? No. Key performance indicators (KPIs) are rarely imposed and there are no rewards and recognition for managing Information Assets effectively. We're finding people with just masses of information in their personal drives, just because they've never been told not to put stuff there.

We further explore leadership and management in Chapter 8.

Domain 5: Information Asset Environment

The Information Asset governance and management domain interprets the business environment in terms of Information Asset governance, of ownership, of strategy, principles, policy and work instructions, of security and privacy, and of the instruments required to manage the organisation's Information Assets. Whereas the business environment domain addresses the enterprise, the Information Asset domain addresses the governance and management of this critical business asset.

> With committed leadership and management (Domain 4), an effective Information Asset governance and management environment including policies and other instruments will be diligently implemented and adherence with them encouraged, thereby creating an effective Information Asset management environment. With an effective Information Asset management environment (Domain 5), information systems are more likely to be fit for purpose (Domain 6).

My firm spends a lot of time looking for information.

My firm is like a library with no index; you don't know where to start finding something and you can search around forever.

We further explore the Information Asset environment in Chapter 9.

Domain 6: Information Technology

The information technology domain represents the technical and physical objects and instruments (hardware, software and networks) required to deliver the right information to the right people at the right time. It addresses the physical assets associated with the management of Information Assets.

With the right Information Asset governance and management (Domain 5), the information technology is more likely to be used efficiently and effectively. For example, the information environment will stipulate clear language and storage location resulting in a single source of truth/system of record. In turn, usable and fit-for-purpose information technology (Domain 6) will support good Information Asset management behaviours (Domain 7).

Information technology pervades and supports almost every aspect of our lives. It is increasingly critical to our existence and well-being. Well-conceived, designed, installed and implemented IT systems increase our productivity, health, safety and wealth. On the other hand, poorly implemented IT systems that are not fit for purpose just get in the way. They are clunky, slow, frustrating and don't do the job they should. People waste time and don't go home to their families when they should. They are massively expensive, not only in the cost of infrastructure but in the cost of managing the information therein. People create workarounds just to get their job done. The following was said by a CEO of a recruitment company and a CIO of a state Department of Health, respectively:

> We have a database system that does not really work and also inadequate software. It's clunky, it's slow, it's excessively manual in its data input and so forth. We can visualise a system that would be better, but we don't know quite where to find it.
>
> There are some clever engines [...] but I've never really seen anything that produces much of use. It always comes back to the fact that information that's not captured in a structured format becomes very difficult to manage. So, the technology has not been particularly effective.

We further explore executive awareness in Chapter 10.

Domain 7: Information Asset Management Behaviour

The Information Asset management behaviour domain refers to the way people within the organisation work with and manage information. Even with the right tools, measurement approaches and policies, good Information Asset management cannot be sustained unless supported by effective behaviours. Poor behaviours include incorrect naming, metadata profiling, security classification, filing and so on. The result is that the right people are unable to find the information they need at the right time, they use information that is obsolete or wrong and unauthorised people are able to access sensitive information. The business impact is increased inefficiencies, duplication, errors and increased risk. This domain is critical for determining the business impact on the organisation of its Information Asset management practices.

Efficient and effective information systems (Domain 6) support good information asset management behaviours (Domain 7). If systems are difficult to use, people will use them sub-optimally, create workarounds or not use them at all. Good Information Asset management behaviours create high-quality Information Assets (Domain 8).

The Managing Partner of a law firm observed,

I experienced tremendous resistance when I tried to move the company from paper to e-files. It was extraordinary, as we're only talking about three years ago, not ten years ago. There was an incredible amount of glue between the lawyers and their hard copy files.

We further explore Information Asset management behaviour in Chapter 11.

Domain 8: Information Asset Quality

The Information Asset quality domain addresses the quality of the Information Assets in terms of:

- availability (can be found in a timely manner);
- correctness (it matches what it is supposed to be);
- completeness (information is not missing);
- currency (it is not outdated for the intended purpose); and
- relevance or applicability (it is fit for the intended purpose and usefully supports employee research, decision-making and action).

> Good Information Asset management behaviours (Domain 7) create high-quality Information Assets (Domain 8). High-quality information allows these Information Assets to be effectively exploited and leveraged (Domain 9).

As we noted in Chapter 2, you can spend millions on technology, but it's pointless if the quality of the organisation's Information Assets is poor.

We further explore Information Asset quality in Chapter 12.

Domain 9: Information Asset Leverage

The Information Asset leverage domain considers how the organisations' Information Assets are put to work to drive business outcomes and to identify further opportunities.

> High-quality information (Domain 8) allows Information Assets to be effectively leveraged and exploited (Domain 9). An ability to leverage Information Assets demands the ability to recognise the business impact that ensues (Domain 10).

Our research investigated a collaboration between an Indian bank and an Australian insurance company that is selling general insurance products to the savings and loan account holders of the bank. The company's Chief Data Officer asked the Board,

"What does our company do?"

The Board replied, *"We sell insurance".*

"How do you do that?"

They replied, *"We price risk".*

"And how do you price risk?"

"Well, we need to understand a person's context so that we can make a sensible business decision. So, the only asset of any value in this entire organisation is our data and information about our customers".

The Board subsequently offered the incoming CEO a double-digit bonus for meeting data quality objectives and threatened termination for failure. Within a week a bonus of US$1000 was offered to every branch to be equally distributed across all branch employees, for hitting data quality targets on three data elements, namely customer first name, customer last name and customer telephone number. The result was that the quality of the organisation's data went from 68% to between 91% and 93% overnight. At the time of the interview, the insurance company was selling 1.7 million new policies per month!

We further explore executive awareness in Chapter 13.

Domain 10: Justification

The justification domain assesses how information management initiatives are justified and can range from technology-driven projects to continuous improvement in Information Asset management practices with in-built benefits realisation.

> The justification domain assesses how information management initiatives are justified. An ability to leverage and exploit Information Assets (Domain 9) demands the ability to recognise the business impact that ensues. The ability to recognise business impact (Domain 10) enables that impact to be quantified and articulated (Domain 1). The justification domain informs the first domain, namely the business impacts domain. With an appropriate justification model, the benefits from effective Information Asset management can be crystallised and recognised.

Many organisations have shallow justification models, recognising little more than cost reduction as justification for investment. This ignores intangible benefits such as productivity increases and thus fails to incentivise such business improvement.

Few organisations have a justification model that allows the funding of continuous Information Asset management improvement. Organisations do not realise the risk of not managing their Information Assets effectively and there is no catalyst or incentive to act.

If people don't suffer pain, they will not be likely to want to do something differently.

We did a large expansion of one of our plants about two years ago and that was the catalyst to try and pull together plant operating knowledge and customer knowledge. We built a business case for a $15 million investment which was approved, because at that moment they realised how much they did not know.

The Chief Knowledge Officer observed, "Effective Information Asset management is not a priority as it is not going to save someone's life".

The Managing Partner of a law firm said, "We're not running an oil rig where someone's going to get killed if we don't follow the manual".

We further explore justification in Chapter 14.

HOW THE TEN DOMAINS INTERACT

Inherently the ten domains have cause and effect. They are deliberately circular in nature enabling a virtuous spiral from effective Information Asset management. On the other hand, poor outcomes in one domain can typically be traced back through multiple others. Here's a live example:

When speaking at a national conference of the Governance Institute of Australia, I asked the 170 or so attendees:

How many of you work for an organisation that has some sort of information management policy – perhaps a cyber policy, a security policy or a records policy?

Almost every hand went up.

And how many of you work for an organisation in which that policy or policies is/are diligently enforced with good behaviour rewarded and bad behaviour discouraged?

Only two hands went up, both from the Independent Commission Against Corruption in Queensland.

That is a disgrace. You are governance people. But, you are not alone. Our research has told us why this happens. It's because the executive just doesn't care. The executive just doesn't care because nobody is being held accountable. Nobody is being held accountable because the executive is not aware of the importance of the organisation's Information Assets. The executive is not aware because the risks, cost, benefits and value have not been quantified and articulated. The benefits have not been quantified because there is no justification model, or the model goes no further than recognising cost reduction… And round the circle it goes.

The remainder of this book closely examines each of the ten domains.

NOTES

1. Evans, N., & Price, J. 2020. Development of a Holistic Model for the Management of an Enterprise's Information Assets. *International Journal of Information Management*, 54.
2. Ladley, J. 2010. *Making EIM Work for Business – A Guide to Understanding Information as an Asset and Data Governance: How to Design, Deploy and Sustain an Effective Data Governance Program.* Morgan Kaufmann.
3. Evans, N., & Price, J. 2015. Information Asset Management Capability: The Role of the CIO. *The 21st Americas Conference on Information Systems (AMCIS).* Puerto Rico. 13–15 August 2015.

5

What Is the Business Impact of How You Manage Your Information Assets?

INTRODUCTION

In Chapter 4 we:

1. explained maturity models and assessment;
2. discussed the development of the "Holistic Information Asset Management Model" which forms the basis of this book; and
3. explained each of the ten focus areas or domains in the Model.

In this chapter we will explore various types of business impact associated with the management of Information Assets, namely:

- risk;
- cost;
- value;
- benefit; and
- ethics.

There is rarely any point in doing something if it doesn't drive a positive business impact.

EXECUTIVE OVERVIEW

The business impact of Information Asset management can be both positive, in the form of business benefit and negative, in the form of business risk.

 DOI: 10.4324/9781003439141-5

Information Assets can deliver benefits, as they are used by every staff member to do their jobs and drive business outcomes for the organisation. Like all other assets, Information Assets have associated risk, cost, value, benefit and ethical issues. There are two costs associated with information management, namely the cost managing the asset (badly) in the first place, and the additional opportunity cost of work foregone. The value of information is not easily quantifiable, and its value depends on context and use. Ethics is associated with how Information Assets are managed and used, particularly with information like customer data. Ethical issues such as confidentiality and privacy of Information Assets are important considerations for your organisation and for you personally.

Domain 1: Business Impact

The business impact domain describes the impact on an organisation of its Information Asset management practices. We start with the business impact, particularly benefits, because they are what matter most; no initiative should be undertaken if there is no benefit to the organisation of doing so.

An ability to justify legitimate benefits (Domain 10) means they are able to be recognised. If the business impact that Information Asset management practices have on the organisation is recognised and understood (Domain 1), executives will take an interest in managing those assets well (Domain 2).

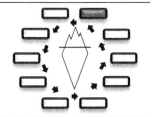

If an organisation is going to continually drive business performance, it needs to continually improve the quality of its Information Assets, and therefore it needs to continuously invest. But no Chief Financial Officer worth his or her salt is going to even look at a business case if they don't believe there is a problem to be solved. They won't approve the business case if the benefits aren't realistic and meet risk mitigation and/or return on investment targets. And they won't reinvest if those benefits aren't recognised and realised.

The business impact domain addresses:

- the risk associated with Information Assets;
- the cost of managing Information Assets;
- the value of Information Assets;

- the realisation of business benefits and improvement of business performance; and
- ethics and professionalism.

WHAT GOOD AND BAD LOOK LIKE

For the business impact domain, this is what good and bad look like:

What good looks like	When Information Assets are managed well, the associated benefits are: • measured; • realised, i.e. they are corroborated; and • recognised, i.e. they are recorded and acknowledged by the Executive.
What bad looks like	The Chief Financial Officer and Board have little idea of: • the risk associated with the organisation's Information Assets or how data, information and knowledge can be deployed to mitigate risk; • what it costs them to manage their organisation's Information Assets (they think it's the cost of hardware, software, upgrades, maintenance, support and IT staff salaries); • the value of their organisation's Information Assets, i.e. how their Information Assets contribute to their organisation's book and market values or the achievement of their business objectives. Benefits are not measured; • the benefit to the organisation of improving the management of its Information Assets; and • the ethical issues associated with their Information Assets and how that are being managed and used.

REALISING BENEFITS AND RECOGNISING BUSINESS IMPACT IS HARD

Realising benefits and recognising business impact isn't easy. In our research, the the CFO of a services organisation commented:

Everybody in this business understands they don't manage their Information Assets well, but they don't know what the benefit is by actually managing them a lot better.

The CFO of a financial institution noted:

> Most people don't like what is nebulous, which is why they struggle with these intangibles.

And a CEO said:

> Although I cannot put a dollar value on information, I can clearly understand the risk and cost of not having the right information at the right time.

In an interview, Doug Laney noted,

- data is not a balance sheet asset;
- most organisations don't measure the performance of their Information Assets – costs, contribution to revenue or benefits, risks or quality;
- you can't manage what you can't measure. And if you can't manage it, you can't drive business benefit from it; and
- a similar lack of measurement or management of other assets would be a dismissible offence.[1]

Doug goes further,

> The business world is starting to wake up, but is not supported by the accounting profession even though data, information and knowledge qualify as assets in that they:

- can be owned and controlled;
- are exchangeable for cash; and
- can drive probable future benefits.[2]

Most organisations don't know:

- what Information Assets they have;
- what risk they face;
- what it costs to manage their Information Assets;
- the value of those Information Assets and to whom;
- the vulnerability of those Information Assets and how they should be protected; or
- what the benefits are of managing them well.

THE TRUCK ANALOGY

Think about physical Assets. They have associated risk, cost, value, benefit and ethics.

Imagine you acquire a new truck. The truck carries **risk**, which can include:

- financial risk – will revenue exceed expenditure or will an accident write off the truck;
- human risk, in terms of lifestyle, injury or death; and
- reputational risk, for example if the truck kills someone.

Risk is defined as the possibility (probability) of exposure to danger, harm or loss. However, there are two sides to risk.

1. On the positive side is opportunity; organisations must take calculated risks in order to advance.
2. On the negative side is threat.

Amongst other measures, the risk associated with the truck can be mitigated through:

- training;
- licensing;
- maintenance; and
- insurance.

The truck comes at a **cost**. The cost of truck can include:

- what you pay for it when you drive it out of the showroom;
- financing costs/interest;
- licensing;
- insurance;
- maintenance;
- fuel; and
- salaries and wages.

The truck has a **value**. The value of an organisation's assets is described as the worth of the assets to stakeholders (customers, employees, trading partners, and community) and their organisation. After 5 years the book value of the truck is zero, having been fully depreciated. Its market value is what someone will pay for a second-hand truck.

The truck has inherent **benefits**, i.e. the money it can make in its productive life, or perhaps the pleasure and pride the one gets from owning and/or driving a truck.

Finally, there are **ethics** associated with owning and driving the truck. For example, is it ethical to drive a truck dangerously fast or whilst under the influence of drugs? To be clear, according to the Oxford Dictionary:

- *morals* are guiding principles of right and wrong, particularly at individual level;
- *ethics* are rules of behaviour, particularly provided by an external source;
- *privacy* is a state in which one is not observed or disturbed by other people,[3] including the right to:
  - be free from interference and intrusion;
  - associate freely with whom you want; and
  - be able to control who can see or use information about you.[4]

Like physical assets, for instance the truck, Information Assets have associated risk, cost, value, benefit and ethics.

Like the truck, Information Assets have associated risks.

- They carry risk in areas including:
  - access and security;
  - disaster recovery and business continuity;

   ○ litigation and discovery;
   ○ compliance;
   ○ competitive advantage;
   ○ human safety;
   ○ personal and corporate reputation; and
  • They can be used to mitigate other business risks. You can't mitigate business risk without the appropriate information.

Information Asset Risk

Access and Security

How do you ensure that you are protecting the right information from the wrong people? How do you manage and protect just that information that is the most valuable. How do you manage and protect that information that is the most vulnerable?

There is a lot of excitement about cyber-security, and with good reason. The implications of a cyber-attack are significant and indicative costs of a cyber-breach are illustrated below in a number of unpleasant examples. However, it is important to keep things in perspective. And once we have perspective, we can take appropriate action. Over the years, the Ponemon Institute has conducted studies for IBM and others into the causes of cyber-security threats (Figure 5.1).

Security threats are growing. However, they don't predominantly come from malicious external actors as we are led to believe.

The 2016 study shows that 22% + 2% = 24% of cyber-security threats are from external sources. Therefore 76% is internal. The 2018 study shows that 48% of cyber-security threats are malicious. Fifty-two per cent is due to

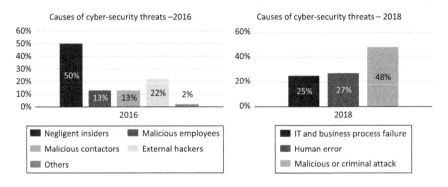

FIGURE 5.1
Causes of cyber-security threats. (*Source*: Ponemon Institute.)

human or other errors. The message here is that there is little point in heaving the problem over the fence to the IT team and expecting them to fix it by installing a firewall. Protection of sensitive data, information and knowledge requires a far more mature and sophisticated approach.

Recent studies at Stamford University have shown that since the COVID-19 pandemic:

- 44% of security incidents were caused by employees;[5]
- more than one-third of all cyber incidents involve internal actors. And over one-third included social engineering;[6]
- 94% of organisations experienced insider data breaches in the last year;[7] and
- 88% of data breaches are caused by human error.

These are important findings because they expose this as a business, not a technology, issue. A new firewall will not do the job.

Security that is too tight can cause problems too. A global defence company views its Information Technology Department as the organisation's "single greatest business inhibitor".

Disaster Recovery and Business Continuity

Some decades ago, an oil and gas company constructed a gas processing plant, the final design of which was recorded in its "as built" drawings. In 2003, corrosion by mercury led to the failure of an inlet manifold and related flange weld which caused an explosion. The organisation was fined $84,000 for breaching the Occupational Health Safety and Welfare Act. Far more expensive, however, was the reconstruction of the plant which was hampered by the inability to find the "as built" drawings. Instead, the burnt and twisted components of the plant had to be retrieved, reverse engineered, produced, transported so that the facility could be reconstructed. An entire floor of the headquarters building was reserved for the legal team. Shareholders were furious.

Litigation and Discovery

The acquisition of a rival by a mining company yielded 80,000 boxes of documentation, one of which contained a pair of working boots and half a cup of coffee casting some doubt on the quality of the information therein and the cost of managing it.

An oil and gas company could not find insurance documentation covering a $100,000,000 accident it suffered when a tug hit an offshore platform.

Compliance

The Australian Taxation Office was prejudiced against an organisation due to its inability to produce a document that was later found elsewhere. Its inability to produce evidence was viewed as non-disclosure.

Having been fined US$400,000,000 an aerospace organisation undertook "to retain an independent compliance monitor". It was also fined £500,000 after admitting it had failed to keep adequate accounting records in relation to the defence contract for the supply of an air traffic control system.

Competitive Advantage

Hackers steal $160 billion worth of intellectual property from western companies every year, according to cyber-security experts. Back in 2015, an Australian communication, metal detection and mining technology firm watched sales and prices of its metal detectors collapse since Chinese hackers stole its designs three years before and sold cheap imitations into Africa.

Human Safety

A Project Manager of an energy generator and distributor gave a site plan to an excavator driver so the driver would know where he could dig. The site plan was a previous version and obsolete. The teeth of the excavator penetrated the plastic coating of an 11,000 volt cable that had been subsequently laid. A centimetre lower and the driver would have been incinerated.

INFORMATION ASSET COST

Like the truck in the analogy above, Information Assets have a cost. As an example, every time a person deals with, say, an email with an important attachment there is a cost in deciding what to call it, where to put it, who to give access to it, how long to keep it for and so on. There is also a cost in finding that document again when required. Every conversation, every meeting, every document, every spreadsheet, every report, every review has a cost. Now some accountants will say that is a salary cost. However, this view assumes either that work practices are as efficient and effective as possible or that productivity is of no interest. Neither view is tenable. The worse Information Assets are managed, the higher the cost in risk, waste, diminished productivity, poorer decision-making and staff frustration.

These costs are significant both in daily operations and when things go wrong.

In daily operations, our anecdotal evidence shows that the waste of poor Information Asset practices alone accounts for more than 20% of a person's day or $20,000 per person per year. We provide a lot of detail and cringeworthy examples later in this chapter.

In Chapters 1 and 2 we discussed assets and liabilities. When things go wrong, it can be really expensive. This is where Information Assets become significant Information Liabilities.

On 22 September 2022 Australia's second largest telecommunications provider became the victim of a cyber-attack that resulted in the disclosure of its customers' personal information.

> With up to 9.8 million Australians having their personal details stolen … customers have started voting with their feet – 10 per cent of those using their mobile service have left the company since the breach … [and] … 56 per cent of current customers [are] "considering changing telcos as a direct result of the cyber-attack", while 10 per cent had already done so, according to the annual EFTM Mobile Phone Survey.[8]

Interestingly, it appears that the cause of the breach was IT using production data in a poorly protected test environment. One wonders whether the breach could or would have occurred if accountability for the quality, protection and exploitation of the organisation's Information Assets had been sheeted home to a single person outside of IT.

On 12 October 2022 a private health insurer suffered a cyber-breach. On 26 October 2022, the *Australian Financial Review* reported that

> about $1.75 billion was wiped off the market value of Australia's biggest health insurer after its shares resumed trading on Wednesday … [The] Chief Executive said the full extent of its remediation and compensation costs for customers would take time to become clear, but put the immediate costs between $25 million and $35 million.[9]

Yesterday, as I write this, the Australian Broadcasting Corporation reported that

Three law firms have joined forces to launch a data breach legal case against [the] health insurance company. This comes after the personal data of about 9.7 million customers was leaked by hackers last year. [Three law firms] have united for the case. The law firms say they will now pursue the complaint seeking compensation for those affected by the data breach.[10]

I can't imagine the shareholders are happy about that.

On 24 March 2023, the *Guardian* reported that 7.9 million drivers licence numbers and 53,000 passport numbers were stolen from a consumer lender which said that some of the documents stolen date back to at least 2005. A further 6.1m customer records were also stolen, of which 5.7m were provided before 2013. These records include information such as names, addresses, phone numbers and dates of birth. The Chief Executive Officer said, "It is hugely disappointing that such a significant number of additional customers and applicants have been affected by this incident. We apologise unreservedly". Shares in the lender dropped more than 3% in a day as traders weighed the potential financial and reputational costs to the company. On 28 March 2023, the *Guardian* further reported that multiple law firms are investigating the viability of legal action and the Minister for Home Affairs is involved.

These breaches raise questions about how companies store data and why many businesses hold on to old customer records. Those records are not assets, they are liabilities, and the cost of those liabilities can be significant. After the breaches described above occurred, in November 2022 the Australian Government passed legislation allowing the Office of the Australian Information Commissioner to seek a penalty of up to $50 million for repeated or serious data breaches. In addition, the lender has promised that it "will reimburse those wishing the replace their stolen ID documents", the market price has dropped, and significant damage has been done to the corporate reputation.

Remember that there are two costs – the cost managing the asset (badly) in the first place, and the additional opportunity cost of work foregone. Think of digging a hole in the wrong place. You have to pay for digging the hole. That is a cost. Then you have to fill in the hole and dig it in the right place. That is an additional cost. And then you have the opportunity cost of work foregone i.e. the work that you could have done if you weren't filling in one hole and digging another.

Until recently a very close personal friend was the Managing Partner of a venerable law firm. A partner of her firm was running a matter in Brisbane. To successfully run the matter, he needed ready access to the firm's information.

So, one weekend he went into the office with a large disc drive and downloaded everything he could. Then he got onto his plane to Brisbane – and lost the drive. The drive had no encryption, no password or any other protection. The Managing Partner lost three months of her life trying to resolve the issue.

A couple of years ago another very close friend who is the owner and Chair of a wool processing operation, identified that his most valuable asset is the corporate knowledge in the heads of his business-critical staff. The Chair embarked on a genuine knowledge management exercise. It was just as well he did. Three months ago, as I write this, the Chief Executive Officer, a man with decades of experience, knowledge and wisdom, died. It was a tragic event for the people around him who loved and respected him. For the business it could have been catastrophic if the owner had not recognised the vulnerability of the business to losing that critical asset.

When considering the costs of managing their Information Assets, most organisations only recognise the costs of delivery, i.e. the IT costs, namely the cost of hardware + software + maintenance + support + upgrades + telecommunications + IT staff salaries. This calculation grossly underestimates the true cost because it only considers the cost of managing the organisation's infrastructure, not the cost of managing its data, information and knowledge.

INFORMATION ASSET VALUE

Like the truck, Information Assets have a value. That value may be calculated through:

- market value;
- replacement value;
- income generating value;
- deprival value; or
- other, or a mix of, methodology(ies).

The value created by intangible assets (such as human capital) prevails over that created by tangible assets (such as machines).

Information Assets have been variously described as:

- "the only meaningful resource";
- "the indisputable value drivers to success";
- "the most important production factor"; and
- "today's driver of company life".

Like the truck, Information Assets have a value, but they are different from most other resources. According to Doug Laney, Information Assets are a

> non-rivalrous, non-depleting asset. The value and return from information ends up being far greater than for other assets. Information is increasingly being substituted for other assets. Uber substituted cars with information and logistics companies substitute just in time information for inventory.[11]

The value of information is not easily quantifiable and its value depends on context and use. Information that has value to an individual one day may not be of value to them the next day; the information ages and may become obsolete. The value is also contextual and user specific. Consolidated information that is valuable to a Chief Executive may not be of the same value to other employees.

The potential value of an Information Asset is not a reliable indicator of its actual value; if the value is never crystallised, there is no benefit to the organisation. The economic value of information often comes from thinking in terms of deprival value, i.e. what would be the consequences if the organisation was deprived of the information.

In his book on "Infonomics"[12] Doug Laney posits six approaches or formulae for calculating the value of Information Assets as follows (Figure 5.2).

Gartner Information Valuation Models

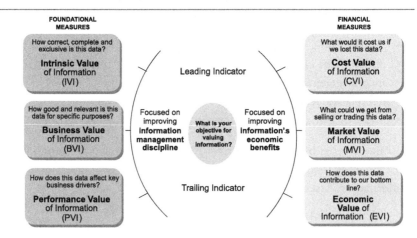

FIGURE 5.2

Information valuation models. (*Source*: Gartner.)

A State government in Australia has expressed interest in valuing its records. It uses a septuagenarian antiquarian to value its hard copy records at $1.5 billion. That does not:

- include its collection of scanned/digitised records;
- include its born digital records; or
- use an intangible asset valuation methodology or a basket of methodologies that would give it a more accurate estimate.

The point here is that there is enormous value in the organisation's Information Assets that is not being leveraged or exploited for business, even State-wide, benefit.

A few years ago, another State government put its Lands Titles Office on the market for $300 million. The asset was sold for $1.065 billion, more than three times its estimated value. Some people will say, "Whacko! We got three times as much as we expected". I am not so bullish because I suspect that we left a lot of money on the table.

A global wine producer has viticultural data that is rich both geographically and longitudinally. Having traditionally and generously given its data away to many organisations for research purposes, the advent of a nascent Agricultural Technology (agtech) company made the wine company realise that its data has real value. It decided to monetise that data.

The wine company identified which of its data is of value to the agtech market; it appointed advisers in data management and quality and in valuing intangible assets; it valued and sold the data; and it identified sources of research funding that could complement the commercial transaction.

The data changed hands in a mutually beneficial transaction. Because the data is now seen by the organisation has having a tangible, realisable value it has attracted the attention of the executive. The commercial details of the transaction are confidential. However, it can be disclosed that the wine company will enjoy a return on the investment in valuing the data of 1,200% over three years. Furthermore, the organisation has a 5-year investment horizon, meaning that it strives to ensure that its projects break even in 5 years. This project broke even in 13 weeks. Not one cent was spent on technology.

INFORMATION ASSET BENEFIT

Like the truck, Information Assets can deliver benefits. They are used by every staff member to do their jobs and drive business outcomes for the organisation.

Experience Matters and the University of South Australia conducted quantitative research involving:

- Chief Operating Officers (COOs) representing 142 North American law firms;
- Information Management (IM) professionals representing 239 mostly government organisations from around the world; and
- 313 staff of a large South Australian State government department (Staff).

From the research findings, the business implications were identified.

Table 5.1 shows the challenges to finding information: 54% of Chief Operating Officers, 62% of Information Management professionals and 43% of the State government department staff nominated not knowing where to look for information. Eighty-two per cent of Information Managers said there are too many places to look and 62% of government agency staff said that poor version control is a problem. And so on.

Table 5.2 shows the types of the business impact of current information management practices that we identified.

Seventy-three per cent of Information Managers identified the inability to comply with legislation as a major implication, 67% of staff of the government agency identified the risk of poor decision-making and, of the COOs of law firms, 65% nominated a potential loss of reputation, 56% a loss of clients and 44% a loss of competitive advantage. These findings constitute serious business risks.

The productivity lost through failing to address Information Asset management practices, or to be gained by improving them, can be seen in Chart 5.1. The chart shows the average avoidable wasted time per week experienced by the staff of a New South Wales State Government department.

TABLE 5.1

Challenges to Finding Information

Challenges to Finding Information	COOs (%)	IM (%)	Staff (%)
Too many places to look	52	82	
Don't know where to look	54	62	43
Not sure of the correct version			62
Too many sources of information		55	58
Constantly changing information			57
Poor navigation			53

(*Source:* Experience Matters)

TABLE 5.2

Business Impact of Information Asset Management

Business Impact	COOs (%)	IM (%)	Staff (%)
Non-compliance		73	54
Poor decision-making			67
Loss of reputation	65	59	32
Litigation		64	
Security exposure			59
Loss of clients	56		
Loss of productivity		52	
Loss of competitive advantage	44		

(*Source:* Experience Matters)

In addition to providing research findings of how Information Assets are managed in two Australian State government organisations, Table 5.3 extrapolates the time wasted to determine the financial impact of poor Information Asset management.

The salary expenses were sourced from the latest available annual report of each organisation. The standard working week is 37.5 hours.

In Organisation 1, $151 million is being wasted per year; the money is being spent for which no service is being received. In 2018 the Australian banking sector was castigated by a Royal Commission for charging fees to people for a

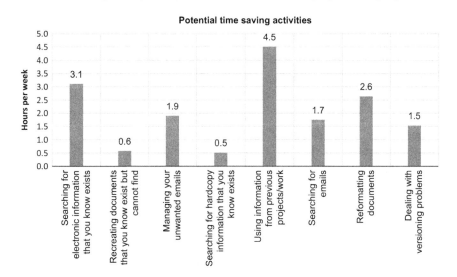

CHART 5.1
Time-saving activities. (*Source*: Experience Matters.)

TABLE 5.3

Financial Impact of Poor Information Asset Management

Description	Organisation 1	Organisation 2
Industry	State government	State government
Number of staff	7,500	150
Staff who know who is responsible for managing the organisation's Information Assets (%)	78	80
Staff who agree there is clear accountability for the management of the organisation's Information Assets (%)	55	42
Staff who are satisfied that their information is complete and accurate (%)	66	70
Staff who are satisfied that their information is current and not out of date (%)	55	70
Staff who believe that productivity would improve through better information management (%)	70	54
Number of potential hours per person per week to be saved (discounted to allow for any potential duplication)	7.8	8.2
Expected benefit	Salaries 2015/16 = $729,000,000 **7.8 h/wk = 20.8% $151,000,000 p.a.**	Salaries 2015/16 = $22,700,000 **8.2 h/wk = 21.9% $4,970,000 p.a.**

(*Source:* Experience Matters)

service that they could not receive because they are dead – an unconscionable and immoral situation. Not only did these figures demonstrate inefficient and ineffective business practices, but they called into question the competence and the ethics of senior managers who failed to run their organisations properly.

Table 5.4 shows the average wasted time by staff.

The estimates by the staff of the South Australian State government agency in Table 5.4 have been savagely discounted for political expediency. By their estimates the average time wasted is closer to 3.88 hours per person per day or more than half their time. Even so, the Chief Executive Officer of the organisation described the estimates of his staff and the findings of the investigation as "rubbish". As of March 2019, the organisation is still paper based; in contrast, IBM Australia went digital in 1985, more than a third of a century ago.

Table 5.5 shows the consolidated findings from numerous organisations across a range of industries. The total estimated waste or potential benefit per

TABLE 5.4

Time Wasted

Effect on Productivity in Hours and Minutes Wasted per Person per Day	COOs	IM	Staff
Searching for or managing unwanted emails	49 min	37 min	35 min
Searching for information they know is there	31 min	47 min	33 min
Recreating documents they know exist	24 min	39 min	19 min
Not using information from previous projects/lessons learned	31 min	36 min	11 min
Total minutes wasted/potential improvement per person per day	135 min	159 min	98 min
Time wasted/potential improvement per person per day	**2 h 15 min**	**2 h 39 min**	**1 h 38 min**
Time wasted/potential improvement per person per week	11 h 15 min	13 h 15 min	8 h 10 min

(*Source:* Experience Matters)

TABLE 5.5

Benefits per Year

Industry	Total Benefit/Year	# Staff	Benefit/Person/Year
Local government	$8,571,000	1,000	$8,571
State government	$155,970,000	7,650	$19,865
Wine	$364,000	34	$10,700
Legal	$1,995,000	150	$13,300
Mining	$24,296,000	1,100	$22,090
Oil and gas	$29,754,000	1,102	$27,000
Totals	**$220,950,000**	**11,036**	**Average $20,021**[a]

(*Source:* Experience Matters)
[a]Total benefit per year divided by total # staff.

year has been divided by the number of staff consulted with to determine the average waste or potential benefit per person per year.

Table 5.6 demonstrates the main identified areas of potential business improvement from better managing Information Assets.

The result is poor information management with: a consequent loss of revenue; an increase in operating cost; the acceptance of waste with its negative effect on productivity; and the impact of risk from inability to meet compliance requirements, compromised cyber-security, ineffective discovery and sub-optimal business continuity. By contrast the benefits of improving the management of Information Assets can be significant and quick to realise.

TABLE 5.6

Opportunity for Improvement

Opportunity for Improvement	COOs (%)	IM (%)	Staff (%)
Improved decision-making		76	62
Increased productivity	70	62	
Improved communication			70
Improved client service	67		47
Higher quality data, better intelligence			63
Improved business performance		51	44
Increased billable hours	44		

(*Source:* Experience Matters)

The examples listed below of operational costs and benefits, both potential and realised, have been identified by Experience Matters as accruing to our clients through the management of their Information Assets; poor information management incurs costs whereas improvements in information management deliver benefits. Costs and benefits can be both tangible and intangible. Tangible costs and benefits are at the client's internal charge-out rates. Intangible costs and benefits are those that cannot be or have not been represented by a dollar figure. The tangible costs and benefits identified by category include the following.

Revenue Foregone

- A global insurance company has approximately 1,000,000 boxes in storage. The contents of 20,000 boxes are unknown, but it is suspected that they contain unprocessed claims representing untapped revenue against other insurance companies worth up to $1,500,000.

Costs Incurred or Saved

- An organisation believes storing inappropriate documents off-site costs $35,000 per year in storage and $20,000 per year in retrieval.
- A mining company used to spend $30,000,000 per year in legal fees, of which between 5% and 25% ($1,500,000 to $7,500,000 per year) was spent on discovery. One action cost $1,200,000 million, of which $300,000 would have been saved if the organisation had found its own documents.

- An organisation believes improved access to documents will enable better defence of insurance claims, reducing annual premiums by $150,000 per year.
- An oil and gas company inadvertently destroyed seismic lines (maps of the sub-surface terrain created with sonar technology and costing approximately $6,000,000 each) because they did not know which of these drawings were the most recent and accurate.
- The inability of an organisation to provide drawings, documents, wiring diagrams, plant dossiers, etc. incurs a surcharge of between 10% and 25% in offshore construction contracts.
- An acquisition by a Malaysian multinational conglomerate included a minority position in an undeveloped oil and gas resource about which it promptly forgot. When the majority owner of the resource decided to develop the resource, the minority owners were informed of their share of development costs and the conglomerate received an unanticipated call for $400,000,000.

Productivity Created or Destroyed

- A mining company has determined that business and mining professionals and managers spend 15 hours per month in avoidable filing, distributing and searching for lost documents. 15 hours × 11 months (excludes holidays) × 589 professionals × $250 per hour (total salary package including on-costs) = $24,296,250 per year.
- Note: This client's internal charge-out rate is too high to be applicable across all organisations. An average salary of $70,000 per year with 30% on-costs constitutes a rate of $52 per hour.
- Another organisation believes some knowledge workers spend up to 50 hours per month looking for documents. Their internal charge-out rate is $150 per hour.
- A consulting engineering firm estimates that if 5 minutes per day is saved, they will achieve a $2,500,000 per year billable productivity improvement. 5 minutes per day × 5 days per week × 48 weeks per year at $50 per hour for 2,500 staff = $2,500,000.
- An oil and gas company with an attrition rate of 22% believes it could reduce the catch-up time of new employees from 8 weeks to 4 with efficient handover. With a staff turnover of 130 people per year and assuming a total salary package of $250 per hour, the opportunity cost is 160 hours × $250.00 per hour × 130 staff = $5,200,000.

- A mining company that lost 152 staff in 12 months calculates that, on average, a new employee wastes 32 hours of his/her time looking for documents. A Senior Manager estimates that he wasted 25% of his time in his first 6 months looking for documents. The organisation's opportunity cost is 152 staff × 32 hours × $150 per hour = $729,600.
- An organisation with approximately 100 staff and an internal charge-out rate of $40 per hour calculated potential savings of $728,000 per year in copying and distribution, retrieval, lost documents, filing and storage.
- An energy utility spent $7,000,000 implementing a well-known electronic records and document management system. The implementation failed because executives did not understand and communicate the value of improving the information and knowledge management of the organisation and users were not told of the benefits of improving the information management practices.
- The Manager of an award-winning winery in McLaren Vale in South Australia decided to apply improvement principles to its data, information and knowledge management. With only 34 staff, the winery needed a pragmatic and cost-effective solution. The organisation:
  - conducted an Information Asset Management Maturity Assessment;
  - extrapolated the business impact upon with winery of its information management practices;
  - developed a business architecture;
  - built a filing plan that matched the activities of the business and was thus intuitive;
  - created naming conventions that used the language of the business;
  - developed email guidelines;
  - implemented these instruments; and
  - developed: a cursory but workable enterprise architecture; a folder structure that, matching the architecture, was intuitive to staff; naming conventions for documents; and email guidelines. Staff now knew what to keep, what to call it and where to put it.
- Shortly after implementation a worker in wine operations enthused, "This is fantastic, we can find stuff". As the organisation could recognise the financial benefit of transforming unproductive activity into productive activity, a benefits realisation programme was implemented. Additionally, network monitoring was set up to see exactly whose behaviour had changed so good practice could be rewarded.

- $91,000 worth of benefit was driven by the winery's 34 staff members using their simple tools in three months, equating to a recurring benefit of $10,800 per person per year without a cent being spent on hardware and software infrastructure. The organisation, which has a 5-year investment horizon, broke even in 8 (actual) weeks. The Winery Manager declared, "There is no other project in our entire investment portfolio that could have delivered a greater return more quickly with better staff satisfaction". That is what we get out of bed for.

- An energy company successfully implemented a business solution, not on the basis of the diligently created business case that articulated productivity improvements but on its ability to reduce unpaid overtime and to send its staff home on time. Needless to say the initiative was welcomed and embraced.

- A government-owned financial corporation used to take days to find the information required to respond to Freedom of Information and Ministerial requests. Since improving its information management, the organisation can now respond in hours and the CFO can personally respond in minutes. Additionally, past employees complain that the environments in which they now work are painfully inferior.

Credibility Enjoyed or Embarrassment Suffered

- A multinational mining company almost lost an asset worth $300,000,000 because a document was not lodged on time. A junior explorer registered its ownership of the tenement for approximately $1,800 and fought to retain its rights. The tenement was returned to the original holder, but only after Ministerial intervention and a High Court decision resulting in plentiful media coverage and extreme embarrassment for the Board and Senior Leadership Team.

- On 31st January 2018, it was reported that the Department of Prime Minister and Cabinet (PM&C) had ordered an urgent investigation into an unprecedented leak of hundreds of top-secret and highly classified cabinet documents discovered in two, locked, second-hand filing cabinets sold off at a Canberra auction house charged with selling ex-government furniture. Within 48 hours three Prime Ministers had weighed in, the one who had ordered the investigation, a second who declared that "heads must roll" and a third who instigated legal proceedings.

Paper Reduction

- An exploration and production company with approximately 900 knowledge workers and 9,000 linear metres (10 linear metres per person) of hard copy material relocated to a new building. A hard copy reduction project was undertaken in which 24% of 9,000 metres was destroyed, 22% was identified for archiving and 6% had no owner. In total, a 52% potential reduction was achieved. The space saved, costed at a rate of approximately $400 per m² per year (worth $1,827,000 per year) is now used for break-out, meeting and collaboration spaces and more effective workspaces and storage.
- A local council was able to reduce document storage costs by 73% and reduce business risk by rationalising storage providers and reducing holdings of paper documents.
- A financial institution reduced its paper holdings excluding the central compact storage from 1306 lineal metres of paper by 598.5 lineal metres to 707.5 lineal metres, a reduction of 45.8%.
- An energy company reduced its paper holdings by 55% with the attendant reduction in costs.
- In reducing its paper holdings, a financial institution was able to hand back two floors of its Sydney building saving over $1,000 per m² per year.

INFORMATION ASSET ETHICS

Like the truck, ethics is associated with how Information Assets are managed and used, particularly with information like customer data. Ethical issues such as confidentiality and privacy of Information Assets are burgeoning topics globally.

Daragh OBrien is co-author of *Ethical Data and Information Management* and founder of Castlebridge, an Irish consultancy. Daragh tells us that ethics is the study of moral behaviour and direction, how people interact with ethical questions and how we frame decision-making. Our ethics are grounded in our culture and social origins, and they go beyond what is right and wrong. Ethics change over time, for instance, at one stage it was considered morally right to curtail the rights and freedoms of people i.e. slavery. Our ethics are also contextual; as an example, whilst aviation fuel can be used to carry food aid to starving people, it can be used to carry bombs.[13] Ethics are also personal. *"Organisations don't have ethics; people do".*[14]

Behaviours have ethical implications at both individual and enterprise levels. You personally might be a victim of hacking or ransomware, or you might be a perpetrator. Organisations might suffer brand damage from poor ethical behaviour.

Causes of unethical behaviour could include:

- your upbringing;
- your personal ethical and moral framework; or
- organisational culture including:
  - ○ customer service,
  - ○ the profit motive,
  - ○ governance structures, and/or
  - ○ management.

With regard to the ethics and privacy in the management of Information Assets, ***data ethics*** describe a code of behaviour, specifically what is right and wrong, encompassing the following.

- *Data Handling:* generation, recording, curation, processing, dissemination, sharing and use.
- *Algorithms:* AI, artificial agents, machine learning and robots.
- *Corresponding practices:* responsible innovation, programming, hacking and professional codes.[15]

Data privacy is the right of a citizen to have control over how their personal information is collected and used.[16]

Data protection is a subset of privacy. Protecting user data and sensitive information is a first step to keeping user data private.[17]

With regard to the management of Information Assets, we need to consider:

- the ethics of identity, for how Facebook, LinkedIn and location tracking are being used and exploited and the ethics of hardship and how it is managed, for instance is it ethical for insurance companies to charge higher insurance premiums for people who live in postcodes that suffer from lower incomes and higher crime rates;
- how information can be used ethically to benefit mankind; and
- how we can maximise business benefit whilst minimising harm.

[Directors] must develop the data and privacy literacy to be able to understand how to discharge their responsibilities and when to ask for expert advice.[18]

Directors and Boards are responsible for directing their entity to leverage data-driven opportunities while ensuring that privacy is built into its governance, control and management. To do less risks both loss of business opportunity and non-compliance with the law.[19]

Risk

- What is the risk to your organisation from poor Information Asset management of:
  - being destroyed by more aggressive competitors that use their Information Assets more effectively?
  - losing your Intellectual Property and vital corporate knowledge?
  - sustaining reputational damage from bad decisions, malicious external actors or inadvertent employees?
  - being unable to recover from a disaster, initiate or defend litigation or comply with the requirements of your legislative and regulatory environment?
  - poor decision-making, ineffective communication, high levels of frustration and low staff satisfaction?
- If you don't know the risk inherent in your Information Assets, how can you be sure that you are properly protecting them?
- What do you need to do to protect your valuable and vulnerable Information Assets?

Cost

- What is the cost to your organisation of managing your Information Assets?

- What is the cost and waste to the organisation of answering unwanted emails, searching for information you can't find, but you know is there and making mistakes caused by having the wrong information?

Value

- What is the value of your Information Assets:
  - to you?
  - to your competitors?
  - to a hacker?

Benefit

- What is the benefit to your organisation from good Information Asset management? How much can your organisation:
  - increase revenue?
  - lower costs?
  - increase productivity?
  - improve speed-to-market (faster, cheaper, higher quality product development)?
  - improve customer delivery and service?

Ethics

- What is the organisation's strategy for protecting privacy?
- How is the organisation's privacy performance measured?
- What measures do you have in place to manage your Information Assets ethically?
- What is the impact of poor-quality information on your organisation's ability to make ethical decisions?

General

- How are the business impacts of poor-quality information calculated?
- How are these business impacts realised and crystallised and, more importantly, recognised and recorded, so that they can be addressed?

NOTES

1. Interview Doug Laney, 12th April 2022.
2. Interview Doug Laney, 12th April 2022.
3. Oxford Dictionary.
4. Office of the Australian Information Commissioner. Available at: https://www.ag.gov.au/about-us/publications/budget-2019-20/portfolio-budget-statements-2019-20/office-australian-information-commissioner.
5. IDG Security Priorities Study. 2021. Foundry. Available at: https://f.hubspotusercontent40.net/hubfs/1624046/R-ES_SecurityPriorities_02.17.22.pdf.
6. Nixu Annual Report. 2021. Available at: https://www.nixu.com/release/nixu-annual-report-2021.
7. Egress Insider Data Breach Survey. 2021. Available at: https://www.egress.com/media/4kqhlafh/egress-insider-data-breach-survey-2021.pdf.
8. News.com.au. 31 October 2022. 10 Per Cent of Optus Customers Leave after Cyberattack. Available at: https://www.news.com.au/finance/business/other-industries/10-per-cent-of-optus-customers-leave-after-cyberattack/news-story/431a0661233a698eb3a6d2bb7c68562c.
9. Australian Financial Review. 26 October 2022. Available at: https://www.afr.com/companies/financial-services/medibank-breach-to-hit-substantially-more-customers-20221026-p5bsxs.
10. News. 17 January 2023. Law Firms Launch Data Breach Legal Case against Medibank. How Will It Work and Who Will Benefit? Available at: https://www.abc.net.au/news/2023-01-17/medibank-hack-data-breach-complaint-explainer/101858182.
11. Interview Doug Laney, 12th April 2022.
12. Laney, Douglas B. 2018. *Infonomics: How to Monetize, Manage and Measure Information As an Asset for Competitive Advantage.* Routledge: New York.
13. Interview Daragh OBrien, 2nd February 2022.
14. Interview Peter Worthington-Eyre, Chief Data Officer, Government of South Australia, 2nd May 2022.
15. Michelle Knight. 19th May 2021. What Is Data Ethics? Dataversity. Available at: https://www.dataversity.net/what-are-data-ethics/.
16. Michelle Knight. 19th May 2021. What Is Data Ethics? Dataversity. Available at: https://www.dataversity.net/what-are-data-ethics/.
17. Michelle Knight. 19th May 2021. What Is Data Ethics? Dataversity. Available at: https://www.dataversity.net/what-are-data-ethics/.
18. Damien Manuel, Chair, Australian Information Security Organisation.
19. Crompton & Trovato. 2018. The New Governance of Data and Privacy. Australian Institute of Company Directors. Available at: https://www.aicd.com.au/good-governance/data/technology/new-governance-data-privacy.html.

6

How Important Is Executive Awareness?

INTRODUCTION

In Chapter 5 we explored the various types of business impact associated with the management of Information Assets, namely:

- risk;
- cost;
- value;
- benefit; and
- ethics.

We saw that managing Information Assets well can deliver very significant tangible, positive business outcomes whereas managing them badly can carry unacceptable risk and have unpleasant consequences.

In this chapter we will look at why the executive's awareness of the importance of Information Assets to their organisations is critical to how those Information Assets are managed and the business implications that ensue.

EXECUTIVE OVERVIEW

The executive awareness domain assesses the extent to which the Board and Senior Leadership Team are aware of, and advocate the importance of, their Information Assets. Without that awareness, nobody will be held accountable for the quality of those assets and the positive business impact enjoyed by all stakeholders from

DOI: 10.4324/9781003439141-6

managing them well. If nobody is held accountable, then nobody will enforce the corporate discipline required for the establishment of a successful and effective Information Asset management environment. Without awareness the executive may not even provide their active support. A lack of executive awareness of the value that can be driven from managing Information Assets well is widespread and has been found in organisations in all industries and countries.

DOMAIN 2: EXECUTIVE AWARENESS

The executive awareness domain assesses the extent to which the Board and Senior Leadership Team are aware of, and advocate the importance of, their Information Assets.

If the business impact that Information Asset management practices have on the organisation is clearly recognised and understood (Domain 1), executives will take an interest in managing those assets well. If they are aware of, and understand, the importance of their Information Assets and how they are governed and managed (Domain 2), they will impose effective business governance conducive to managing those assets well (Domain 3).

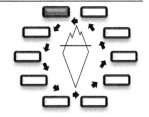

As we will explore in the next chapters, without that awareness, nobody will be held accountable for the quality of those assets and the positive business impact enjoyed by all stakeholders from managing them well. If nobody is held accountable, then nobody will enforce the corporate discipline required for the establishment of a successful and effective Information Asset management environment. Without awareness the executive may not even provide their active support.[1]

In Chapter 3 we explained that many executives are unaware of the value of their Information Assets and the importance of managing them well. Anecdotal evidence and research findings show that there is:

- a lack of formal, particularly tertiary, postgraduate and executive education, in that;
    - o secondary schools provide lessons in programming and software development. They teach the fundamentals of economics. But nothing is taught in secondary schools about business and the assets that organisations use,

○ universities get excited about the shiny things, but not the important things, and

○ executive education is still missing the mark. Few, even respected, board and executive networks and associations have taken any interest in the management of data, information and knowledge, with the exception of cyber-security which usually has a highly technical, infrastructure-based focus. The Governance Institute of Australia is a notable exception, and

• little on-the-job education. Some organisations train new employees in their induction, but few organisations provide education on a continuing basis.

In Chapter 4 we mentioned that, whilst presenting to a national conference, I asked attendees whether their organisations had some sort of Information Asset management policy and whether that policy had been well implemented. To be effective, polices need to be properly implemented, and that requires communication and education. However, good Information Asset management requires far more than well-implemented policies. It requires the development of a culture of valuing, governing and managing data, information and knowledge as a vital business asset.

What is required is:

• a deep understanding of the risks, costs, value, benefits and ethics associated with the organisation's Information Assets;
• communication of corporate expectations;
• education; and
• training.

WHAT GOOD AND BAD LOOK LIKE

For the executive awareness domain, this is what good and bad look like:

What good looks like	The Board and executive deeply understand the value and importance of the organisation's Information Assets and demand their effective governance and management.
What bad looks like	The Board and executive have no interest in managing their data, information and knowledge as a strategic business asset. Unlike the Financial Statements, Information Asset management is not a Board agenda item, and the Board does not know what hard questions to ask the executive.

In the case of our "what good looks like" exemplar, the titular head of the organisation declared, "Information will be our legacy". And the Executive Director, who is effectively the Chief Executive of the organisation, called the initiative the "Everybody's Information System". These blokes understand the importance of their Information Assets and they are leading from the top. Brilliant.

In the case of our "what bad looks like" exemplar, remember that this is the organisation with the stated objective of creating "a high-performing organisation of excellence" with "an innovative, agile and collaborative workforce" that "delivers effective and efficient public services" to "its key clients, including [the agency's] employees, the [agency's] executive, [its] ministers and central government agencies". We proposed executive awareness and education as one of the very first projects in the programme of work. We also proposed realising, measuring and recognising the benefits enjoyed by the organisation from managing its Information Asset well.

About six months into the initiative, things were not going well, to say the least. We ran a badly delayed programme of awareness creation to the project team and the very few business people that the project team had engaged. Upon completing the awareness exercise, they declared, "You must run this awareness creation for the executive!" Did they do it? No. Did they conduct the benefits realisation? No.

Another terrific example is one of the Australian State government agencies described in Chapter 5. We explained that the expected benefit of improving the management of its Information Assets was found to be at least $151,000,000 per year. We showed that this figure is calculated, admittedly simplistically, as follows:

$ 729,000,000	Annual employee-related expenses 2015/16
× 20.8%	Expected productivity improvement of 7.8 hours per 35-hour week
= $151,000,000	Expected benefit per annum

These are not our numbers; they are theirs. And they are conservative. The findings went precisely nowhere. Perhaps here's why:

7,500 staff
188 of 3,508 eligible staff consulted with
4 (2.1%) of executives consulted with

There was zero interest from the executive, zero engagement, support or encouragement of and by the business, and zero action taken as a result of the findings. If I were a taxpayer of that State, I would be livid.

A third example is of a State government department that anecdotally:

- prematurely released 36 prisoners back into the community and incarcerated one person for 5 years longer than they should have;
- manages its cases in Microsoft Calendar; and
- includes in the job descriptions of the eight staff in its Information Management team, "answering telephones, filling photocopiers with paper and removing staples".

An Information Asset Management Maturity Assessment was commissioned that found that 3.88 hours per person per day is wasted. That equates to 19.4 hours or 51% of each person's working week. Extremely conservatively, if it managed its Information Assets well, the agency would enjoy a business benefit of over $18,350,000 per year.

Of the additional benefits to be enjoyed from improving Information Asset management practices, 70% of respondents indicated that communication would be improved whilst 62% nominated higher quality data and better intelligence, followed by community, staff and offender safety (47%) and improved business efficiency (44%). Of the risks to be mitigated from improved Information Asset management, 67% of staff identified poor decision making and 59% indicated security exposures, followed by non-compliance (54%), incidents in custody (34%) and loss of reputation (32%).

A lack of executive awareness of the value that can be driven from managing Information Assets well is not confined to the public sector. A mining company with 589 staff conducted a maturity assessment. Its findings showed that the organisation could drive nearly $24 million per year in business improvement. The Chief Executive asked,

- What's that based on?
- Productivity improvements.
- Excellent. Who can I sack?
- Nobody.
- In that case your business case doesn't stand up. Get out of my office.

Supporting the anecdotal evidence above, our research findings show that executives view data, information and knowledge as a vital business asset, yet they do not understand how these assets should be managed and they need to be convinced of the benefits of effective management of those assets.

The problem is not recognised. Organisations do not realise the risk of not managing their Information Assets effectively.

> I am not sure, even in my own mind, that there is a problem to solve, as a problem implies that there's downside based on the way that the organisation is working now.

The Managing Partner of an Australian law firm commented:

> We are sub-optimal for every day that we are not managing [information] as well as it could be, we're sub-optimal, but does that mean we've got a problem? Not necessarily.

There is very little formal training in the management of Information Assets. There is a lack of formal, particularly tertiary, postgraduate and executive, education; and little on-the-job education and induction. The CIO of a transport company commented:

> I have just completed my MBA and I learnt about everything – strategy, risk, governance, finance, IT, HR, the works, but not a word was spoken about the management of information.

The CEO of a manufacturing organisation confirmed that when he did an MBA "IT was a part of the curriculum so you wouldn't look stupid talking to an IT professional". He added, "It [Information Management] is not yet a recognised discipline. People confuse it with information technology, which is not information management".

The Chief Financial Officer of an Automotive Services organisation commented that the Australian Director's courses have an IT component and a Finance component, but there is nothing about managing information.

A CIO mentioned that managers are removed from the management of Information Assets the further they move up the management chain.

Further, a Board member referred to information as "an amorphous concept that is like a handful of jelly" and added that people do not know what it is, how to manage it and what the key performance indicators (KPIs) are.

The problem for executives is how to quantify and visualise risk and opportunity associated with their most valuable and vulnerable asset. This exercise is crucial if the asset is to be managed properly. We discuss this further in Chapter 14: Justification.

- How aware is the executive of your organisation of the risk, cost, value and benefit inherent in its Information Assets?
- How is this awareness (or lack of awareness) manifested?
- If an aggressive competitor wanted to destroy you, what would they need to do that?

NOTE

1. Evans, N., & Price, J. 2015. Enterprise Information Asset Management: The Roles and Responsibilities of Executive Boards. *Knowledge Management Research and Practice* advance online publication. March 10, DOI: 10.1057/kmrp.2014.39.

7

Why Is the Governance and Management of Your Business So Important?

INTRODUCTION

In Chapter 6 we looked at why the executive's awareness of the importance of Information Assets to their organisations is critical to how those Information Assets are managed and the business implications that ensue.

In this chapter we will:

- discuss the difference between accountability and responsibility, as well as between governance and management;
- highlight their critical importance to creating a business environment that is conducive to managing Information Assets well; and
- examine the role of the Board and Chief Executive in assigning accountability and responsibility to the appropriate stakeholders to manage Information Assets well.

Understanding these differences is critical. Most organisations have some sort of data and information governance, but the evidence shows that it is pointless without the support of good business governance.

EXECUTIVE OVERVIEW

An organisation's governance and management dictate how its activities are conducted and its resources are deployed. Governance refers to what

DOI: 10.4324/9781003439141-7

decisions must be made and who makes those decisions to ensure effective management. Business (corporate) governance provides oversight and control of the organisation as a whole entity, whereas asset governance provides oversight and control of a specific asset. Whilst Boards and Chief Executives often recognise their role in making somebody accountable for the governance and management of their financial (money) and physical assets, they do not recognise that Information Assets are just as important. A lack of business governance was identified in our research as an important reason why organisations are not successful in managing their Information Assets.

DOMAIN 3: BUSINESS ENVIRONMENT

The business environment domain addresses the governance and management of the enterprise as a whole. It considers the organisation's business governance that typically addresses "who makes what decisions". This is the level above the organisation's asset governance and management.

If the Board and Chief Executive Officer are aware of the importance of effective Information Asset management (Domain 2) they will impose effective business governance conducive to managing those assets well (Domain 3). If the organisation is governed well, its leaders and managers will lead by example and create a culture of managing Information Assets well (Domain 4).

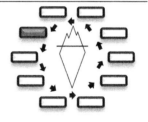

In Chapter 1 we noted what executives are interested in at the enterprise level. In Chapter 4 we explained our Holistic Model which is represented by an iceberg. Above the water line are the business focussed domains whereas below the line are the Information Asset management domains. The business environment domain addresses the organisation's:

- corporate and/or departmental purpose, vision, mission, goals and objectives;
- corporate strategy and how those goals and objectives will be achieved;
- functions and the processes by which its business activities are conducted;

- capability as evidenced by the resources they have available through which they conduct those activities and processes;
- method of governing, managing and deploying those resources to drive the greatest value and probability of success; and
- culture and language.

GOVERNANCE AND MANAGEMENT

An organisation's governance and management dictate how its activities are conducted and its resources are deployed. In Chapter 1 we noted that governance and management are different. To illustrate, we will examine the asset that is governed and managed best by all organisations, namely money.

The Governance Institute of Australia defines governance as "the system by which an organisation is controlled and operates, and the mechanisms by which it, and its people, are held to account. Ethics, risk management, compliance and administration are all elements of governance". Governance refers to what decisions must be made (decision domains) and who makes those decisions (locus of accountability for decision-making) to ensure effective management (executing the decisions).[1,2] Governance is about oversight and control. It is about doing the right things.[3] Management refers to actually making and implementing decisions, particularly regarding the deployment of resources.[4] Management is about driving business value through execution. It is about doing things right. The distinction between governance and management applies to all decision domains, including decisions related to data, information and knowledge.

There are (at least) two levels of governance, namely business governance and asset governance. Business governance provides oversight and control of the organisation as a whole entity, whereas asset governance provides oversight and control of a specific asset.

Business Governance

Business governance applies at the highest business level. The Board and Chief Executive Officer decide who makes what decisions regarding the overall business. They make a single person accountable for managing and leveraging a specific asset in different parts of the business – the person at whom the buck stops for that asset. Accountability is defined as, "the liability to ensure that a task is satisfactorily done".[5] In the case of Financial Assets, the Board and Chief Executive appoint a Chief Financial Officer (CFO) and they make that person accountable for the asset. A critical role of business governance is therefore to monitor and control the behaviour of senior executives, who deploy the assets at their disposal and manage the organisation.

Asset Governance

Unsurprisingly asset governance applies at the asset level; it is accountability for specific assets. The CFO is accountable for the governance of the organisation's Financial Assets. (S)he provides oversight and control of that specific part of the business. Amongst many other tasks, the Chief Financial Officer develops the finance strategy, determines the annual budget and develops and maintains the frameworks (Chart of Accounts) and instruments (Balance Sheet, Income Statement, Cash Flow Analysis) by which the asset is managed. (S)he delegates responsibility and authority to a carefully selected group of managers to spend an agreed amount of money for an agreed purpose over an agreed time frame. And (s)he reports to the Chief Executive Officer (and ultimately Board) on the deployment of organisation's Financial Assets. The CFO will be sacked if (s)he mismanages the organisation's money and will be jailed if (s)he misappropriates it. There is true accountability for this asset. The buck (yuk, yuk, yuk) genuinely stops with them. The same approach applies to other parts of the business such as human resources (Human Resource Manager) and physical resources (Site Manager/IT Manager).

MANAGEMENT

Management involves making and implementing the decisions.[6] Management is about driving business value through execution. It is about doing things right.

The Chief Financial Officer provides asset governance, not management. Management of the Financial Assets is done by the people who have been given the authority or delegation and responsibility to spend a certain amount of money for a certain purpose within a certain time. They are responsible for spending the money and ensuring that the organisation gets value for the expenditure. Responsibility is defined as, "the obligation to satisfactorily perform a task".[7]

Asset Management

The Australian Asset Management Council defines asset management as, "the life cycle management of physical assets to achieve the stated outputs of the enterprise". This definition makes no mention of Intangible Assets. The Oxford definition is succinct, "the active management of assets in order to optimise return on investment".

Table 7.1 summarises the relationship between business governance, asset governance and asset management for asset types typical of most organisations.

So how is money managed? Money has a framework called the Chart of Accounts. Without it, expenditure can be allocated indiscriminately and to multiple uses so reporting and management would be impossible. Money is managed and reported on through financial instruments such as the Balance Sheet and the Income Statement.

The same is true for Human and Physical Assets, as per Table 7.2.

Few organisations have a formal framework for managing their Information Assets and, if they do, they don't understand them. Most executives don't understand what a Business Classification Scheme is let alone its profound strategic value. A Business Classification Scheme can be thought of as an Information Chart of Accounts; it is the Information Assets equivalent of the Financial Chart of Accounts for Financial Assets. Most organisations have at least a few tools for managing Information Assets throughout their lifecycle, but as we noted in Chapter 4, developing an Information Asset management policy does not mean it will be implemented with good Information Management behaviour rewarded and bad behaviour discouraged. Most importantly, few organisations have an executive truly accountable, i.e. able to be sacked, for the quality of the organisation's data, information and knowledge.

The Importance of Business Governance

Without somebody being held accountable, nobody is going to delegate responsibility. And without responsibility being delegated, the leadership, management and staff of the organisation simply won't care. It's not their job and it therefore won't be done.

TABLE 7.1

Governance

	Business Governance	**Asset Governance**	**Asset Management**
Activity	Oversight of and control over the business. Decides who makes what decisions, i.e. who will be accountable for a nominated asset. Doing the right things at the business level.	Oversight of and control over a nominated asset i.e. develops the strategy, policy, instruments, measurement and reporting. Doing the right things at the asset level.	Day-to-day management of the asset. Makes the decisions and implements them. Doing things right.
Accountability versus responsibility	Accountability. Where the buck stops for the business.	Accountability. Where the buck stops for the asset. Typically, a single individual.	Responsibility. Can be shared by many people.
By	Board – Chair and business – CEO.	Financial Assets – CFO. Human Assets – CHRO. Physical Assets – Site Manager, IT Manager Intangible Assets –?	Those with delegated authority.
Reporting	Financial Assets – CEO reports to the Board with financial reports.	The person accountable for the asset reports to the CEO.	Financial Assets – Finance Department reports on revenue, expenses, etc. Human Resources – HR Department, etc.

(*Source*: Experience Matters)

However, whilst Boards and Chief Executives recognise their role in making somebody accountable for the governance and management of their physical assets, they do not recognise that Information Assets are just as important. A conversation with a Director went as follows:

Question: Have you ever been involved in appointing people specifically to manage information and knowledge in organisations?

Answer: No ... it's not the board's job to do that.

TABLE 7.2

Frameworks, Tools, Responsibility and Accountability for Assets

Asset	Framework	Tools	Responsibility	Accountability
Financial	Chart of Accounts	Balance Sheet Income Statement	Delegated authority	CFO
Human	Organisation Chart	Roles & Responsibilities KPIs	Line management	Director HR
Physical	Asset Register	Maintenance and Improvement Programmes	Delegated authority	Property Manager Site Manager IT Manager
Intangible	Business Classification Scheme	Metadata model Security model Retention schedule	Everybody??	Nobody??

(*Source:* Experience Matters)

WHAT GOOD AND BAD LOOK LIKE

For the business environment domain, this is what good and bad look like:

	Business governance	Asset governance	Management
What good looks like	Accountability for the effective management of the organisation's assets has been clearly imposed upon a single individual and their job depends upon delivering the asset vision and objectives. Those accountable are measured and rewarded for their performance. A Chief Financial Officer will be sacked if (s)he mismanages the organisation's money and jailed if (s)he misappropriates it.	Data, information, content and knowledge are governed as a strategic business asset. Those accountable measure and reward their staff on their performance. Information Asset management principles, strategy, policy, guidelines and instruments are effective, maintained and used/adhered to.	Management and staff are measured and rewarded on their Information Asset management performance, particularly the quality of the Information Assets for which they are responsible. There is a culture of understanding the value of, caring for, and leveraging the organisation's Information Assets.

What bad looks like	Nobody is accountable for the management of the organisation's vital assets. Nobody is interested in ensuring asset management policies are adhered to and behavioural expectations are met.	The ownership of, and responsibility for IAs is unclear and defaults to IT whose KPIs are centred on throughput and uptime, not on IA quality. The IA lifecycle and its management are not understood, and instruments including policy and agreed corporate language are neither developed nor implemented.	Management and staff don't care about their Information Assets. Those responsible for the management of Information Assets have job descriptions that include tasks of "answering telephones, filling photocopiers with paper and removing staples" (these are real examples). There are multiple versions of information in multiple repositories called multiple things. The right people can't find the information they need at the right time.

BUSINESS FRAMEWORKS

Organisations have frameworks with which they manage their assets. They have Charts of Accounts, Organisation Charts and Asset Registers. The most effective frameworks match the business. By building them to match the business, frameworks are:

- intuitive because the frameworks reflect what the organisation does; and
- stable, because the business of an organisation itself is usually slow to change. In Experience Matters' case, its business has not materially changed in more than two decades; the organisation has always been a firm of advisers in the management of Information Assets.

An Australian mining company was purchased to briefly create the largest of its type in the world. The incoming Australasian Managing Director realised that we had helped them map their business activities in order to create a matching framework for their data, information and knowledge assets. He asked us to reconcile the organisation's global Chart of Accounts with the Business Activities Map. He said,

> You have shown me that our global financial Chart of Accounts does not include the activity of Human Safety which is our number one priority. It does not include Environmental Management which is also crucial for a mining company. And it does not include Board Governance. I have concluded that the fundamental framework by which we manage our financial assets does not match our business.

LACK OF BUSINESS GOVERNANCE

A lack of business governance was identified in our research as an important reason why organisations are not successful in managing their Information Assets.

The Board member we introduced in Chapter 3 indicated that, from a Director's perspective, the management of data, information and knowledge is invisible unless something goes wrong.

Director: *From my perspective as a director, you just don't see that [data management is important]. I mean that is unless something goes wrong, that is outside the framework of what we're there for which is setting in place the strategy and oversight of the strategy of the organisation. Now whether this should be included in the oversight you're probably going to tell me, "Yes, I think it should be".*

James: *It's up to you guys to decide that.*

Director: *Well, it's not on the radar.*

James: *Yeah. Now why is it not on the radar?*

Director: *It's not considered to be a big enough risk.*

James: *Because things have just been going along quite happily and so therefore there's no need?*

Director: *Yeah … from a director's point of view, there's two main things we get involved with. One is setting the strategy, an oversight of the strategy. The second thing is when the s..t hits the fan, working out what to do … as* *effectively as possible. This stuff doesn't fit into the strategy and it usually doesn't fit into the s..t because you don't see it. You know if there's a bill from our lawyers for 30 million bucks for a year you ask the question. Why are we paying $30 million a year? Is there a better way of doing it? [Maybe.] But, it's just not on the agenda.*

The Director went further:

[t]he difficulty that you have in this, in developing this as a risk for organisations is making it feel like it's a risk. It doesn't feel like a risk to me.

[Information is] not as graphical as the other [assets]. You misappropriate $1 million, and it comes out. It's $1 million, where is it? You lose a truck, where's the truck? You know, shareholders look at the dollars, the physical assets, the physical liabilities, the generation of wealth, you know [knocking sound] what is here. But this is nebulous.

Then we began to recognise the contradictions:

Everyone manages their information to an extent. Everyone understands how important it is. I mean if we can't find an email that's important at the right time, you start getting a little bit sweaty under the armpits. If it's a really important email, you've got to respond to it or there's dollars hanging off, you get very sweaty.

Clearly articulating accountability at all levels of the organisation will support the appropriate management of Information Assets. An executive from a large bank indicated that there are varying opinions about who is responsible and added "who is responsible hasn't been nutted out of this organisation".

Older people who have done well in their careers and are retiring from their jobs often become non-executive directors. I like to ask them how often they ask to see the financial statements, the report on how well the organisation's financial assets are being managed. They say,

James, you're an idiot. We ask to see Financial Statements every Board meeting, every single month.

And I reply,

Well that's fantastic. And how often do you ask to the Information Statements, the report on how well the organisation's most important resource, its Information Assets, are being managed?"

Silence. And then they say, "What are they?

Remember from the preface that we asked an oil and gas producer what the organisation would look like if it managed its Financial Assets the way it manages its Information Assets. The answer was, "We would be broke in a week". And a Named Equity Partner of a Washington, DC–based law firm said, "We would be out of business by Thursday". In other words, they don't govern and manage their Information Assets at all.

In a positive example, an Australian police force recognises that to combat increasingly sophisticated crime it needs to evolve from being reactive to predictive. It also realises that:

1. to be preventative you need to be predictive;
2. to be predictive you need insights from information;
3. to gain reliable, high-quality insights you need high-quality data;
4. to have high-quality data you need a single source of truth/single system of record;
5. to have a single source of truth you need corporate discipline;
6. to have corporate discipline you need management and incentive; and
7. to have management and incentive you need corporate governance.

- How often does the Board ask to see the Financial Statements – the reports on how well the organisation's Financial Assets are being managed? And how often does the Board ask to see the Information Asset Statements – the reports on how well the organisation's Information Assets are being managed?
- Who is the one person who, like the CFO, is truly accountable for the quality of the organisation's Information Assets?
- What authority does the accountable person have to enforce adherence to corporate Information Asset management principles and standards?
- If your Chief Information Officer was genuinely accountable (i.e. rewarded for success and sacked for failure) for the quality of the

organisation's Information Assets, what would (s)he demand to enable them to be successful?

- If your Chief Information Officer was made genuinely accountable for the accuracy, relevance and timeliness of your organisation's information provision, what would he or she demand?
- If the executive of your organisation does not manage its Information Assets as well as it could or should, what are the reasons for that?

NOTES

1. Evans, N., & Price, J.. *Responsibility and Accountability for Information Asset Management (IAM) in Organisations.*
2. Evans, N., & Price, J. *Managing Information in Law Firms: Changes and Challenges.*
3. John Ladley interview, 10th February 2022.
4. Khatri and Brown. 2010. Designing Data Governance. *Communications of the ACM,* 53(1): 148–152
5. McGrath & Whitty. 2018. Accountability and Responsibility Defined. *International Journal of Managing Projects in Business,* 11(3) :687–707.
6. Khatri & Brown. 2010. Designing Data Governance. *Communications of the ACM,* 53(1): 148–152
7. McGrath, S.K. & Whitty, S.J. 2018. Accountability and Responsibility Defined. *International Journal of Managing Projects in Business,* 11(3): 687–707.

8

What Is the Role of Leadership and Management in Encouraging Good Information Asset Practices?

INTRODUCTION

In Chapter 7 we:

- discussed the difference between accountability and responsibility, as well as between governance and management;
- highlighted their critical importance to creating a business environment that is conducive to managing Information Assets well; and
- examined the role of the Board and Chief Executive in assigning accountability and responsibility to the appropriate stakeholders to manage Information Assets well.

In this chapter we will look at

- the role that leadership and management takes in encouraging good Information Asset management behaviour and discouraging bad practices; and
- how to create the corporate discipline required to manage data, information and knowledge as a strategic business asset.

Without good leadership and management the organisation will never impose the standards and behaviours required for good Information Asset management.

DOI: 10.4324/9781003439141-8

EXECUTIVE OVERVIEW

Leadership and management creates the corporate discipline, management instruments, measurement and incentives required to manage data, information and knowledge as a strategic business asset. Leaders should think about data, information and knowledge on an organisation-wide basis and these assets should be very important to them. Change needs a change champion, a visionary, to lead an organisation through change. That person has to be an executive.

DOMAIN 4: LEADERSHIP AND MANAGEMENT

The leadership and management domain addresses the organisation's human resources, structure, roles, culture, behaviour and incentives regarding the management of Information Assets.

With a conducive business environment (Domain 3), the organisation's leaders and managers will lead by example and create a culture of managing Information Assets well. With committed leadership and management (Domain 4), Information Asset management policies and other instruments will be diligently implemented and adherence with them encouraged, creating an effective Information Asset management environment (Domain 5).

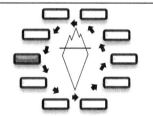

Good leaders and managers will address a range of issues including:

- structure;
- culture and behaviour;
- resources;
- roles;
- measurement

- incentivisation; and
- the ability of the organisation's staff to do the work.

WHAT GOOD AND BAD LOOK LIKE

For the leadership and management domain, this is what good and bad look like:

What good looks like	Driven by measurements such as Key Performance Indicators and associated incentives, and supported by education and training, the organisation's culture ensures that Information Assets are universally appreciated, managed, leveraged and protected the same way the organisation's financial, physical and human assets are.
What bad looks like	At worst, managing Information Assets is seen as a boring administrative overhead and at best as a mere compliance issue. Job descriptions of Information Managers have been found to include tasks like "answering telephones, filling photocopiers with paper, removing staples" and "buying the milk". Good Information Asset management behaviours are not rewarded, and bad behaviours are not discouraged.

Good leadership and management create an environment in which change for the better is encouraged and accepted.[1] As an example of what good looks like, a State Department of Health implemented a Clinical Information System throughout the whole of metropolitan public health in the State – the eight major public hospitals. The Director of Hospital Systems realised that he needed to develop communication strategies and plans to support the $94 million implementation.

The communication programme created greater stakeholder consensus resulting in lower project implementation risk, reduced waste of competing project resources and quicker solution acceptance and adoption providing faster business returns.

The Director of Hospital Systems was subsequently approached, independently and unsolicited, by the CEOs of three hospitals. They requested that the project be documented as a benchmark or case study of how massive software solutions should be implemented. The CEOs had been highly impressed by how each stakeholder group had been consulted and their requirements catered for. Each group knew how it would benefit them.

The CEOs knew how it would affect their risk profile and their bottom line. The doctors knew how it would affect their work at the bedside. The nurses' union knew how it would affect its members' working conditions and the Minister knew how it would affect him politically.

When a newly installed government investigated the project to determine whether it could reduce funding costs, the Minister met with the Department of Health. The Department advised the Minister to consult with people on the front line whom the initiative was meant to be supporting and, if their needs weren't being met, the project could be cancelled. Based on perceived value to the community the project's budget, instead of being reduced, was increased from $94 to $110 million.

As an example of "what bad looks like", Information Asset management policies are written for compliance purposes only and they are left on the digital shelf gathering metaphorical dust. Furthermore, structure and governance aren't imposed, staff aren't trained in the policies or the organisation's expectations, corporate adherence and behaviour are not measured and incentivised, Information Asset management is abdicated to IT and information chaos results.

This brings us to a critical point. How many shareholders know how well the assets of their organisations are being managed? They deeply understand it when there is a cyber breach resulting in a massive loss of share price and market capital. But how many understand what the day-to-day management is costing them? If they knew that, we suspect that they would be deeply unhappy.

We also remember the State government agency, described in Chapter 6, that has a team of eight Information Managers tasked to conduct trivial activities, yet the Department wastes 51% of its entire staff's working time.

The findings of our research have shown that few organisations treat their data, information and knowledge as a strategic business asset. Most of the participants referred to either the Librarian or the Chief Information Officer (IT Manager) as the custodian or manager of their organisations' Information Assets. The problem is that whilst the Librarian is a subject matter expert, understands managing Information Assets well and has authority (s)he lacks seniority. Similarly, whilst the IT Manager has the responsibility for delivering Information Assets to those who need them, (s)he lacks both the subject matter expertise and the authority to maintain high-quality Information Assets.

THERE IS A LACK OF EXECUTIVE SUPPORT

Other than the Board, the Chief Executive Officer (CEO) is often the only person who takes an enterprise view of the company, who cares about the overall performance, and who is concerned with creating sustainable value. The Chief Information Officer (CIO) of a financial institution said:

> The executive views the value of information and knowledge real laissez-faire. I don't think it's something that gets discussed.

The CIO of a local council observed that his organisation lacks Information Asset Management vision.

> The vision and insight do not exist. Organisations do not understand that if they invest [...] more effort in Information Asset management they will see a return on their investment. You get to your five-year term of office and you say, so what did we do the last five years? We were extremely busy but what did we actually do? We did mostly maintenance.

The Data Manager of a financial institution noted,

> We're still not comfortable about the support from the top. There are a lot of good words spoken. A challenge we have at the moment is trying to make sure that at the top they're actually putting their money where their mouth is.

A Manager of another financial institution observed,

> The whole focus is on the tangibles of the business – the hard things that make this business work. It's getting products to market, getting sales, collecting money, investing money and managing expenses.

THERE IS A LACK OF INCENTIVE TO MANAGE INFORMATION ASSETS WELL

Employees only take an interest in what is measured and rewarded. A Director said,

Individuals need to hit their time budgets or deliver their volume of new revenue to the business, so they are not incentivised to collaborate for the greater good of the firm.

The CEO of an Information Services organisation agreed that,

People will manage their budget because they get incentives according to the budget, so they drive it from that perspective.

THE ORGANISATION MUST SHOW STAKEHOLDERS WHAT'S IN IT FOR THEM

The CIO of a law firm said,

We need to show people why improved information management is going to be better for them, not be too directive.

A CFO noted,

Like all organisations, we certainly struggle with it, and we don't bring it to the surface and give it the level of resources that it would need to get that value out. I think if we did understand the value then we'd change our thinking.

Extraordinarily, a CIO of a local council announced,

I have real work to do; I haven't got time to waste on information management.

MANAGERS NEITHER SET EXPECTATIONS NOR LEAD BY EXAMPLE

The Chief Knowledge Officer (CKO) of a utility said that

The MD just assumed that the work we wanted to do was a technical solution, so I've been very careful in all the change communications to show that it's not.

According to the CKO of a government department,

> It can't be shared, it can't be found. If they leave, all the work they've done is sitting on a P drive somewhere.

The CIO of a financial institution said:

> Managers get by on experience, which is why they don't focus on managing the Information Assets. A blessing and a curse is that many of the top management came through the ranks, so they know where the curve balls are, they know where the efficiencies are, and they've learned to make do with those defects. That's how we got so well through the crisis. As far as they're concerned, expert judgment or gut feel still goes a long way to make this good.

CULTURE IS CRITICAL BUT PEOPLE RESIST CHANGE

Change needs a change champion, somebody that's strong enough to pull an organisation through the low parts of the change cycle. That person needs to be a visionary. It has to be an executive.

A CKO said,

> It is not part of people's mindset to think about how information could be used elsewhere by others. That's the culture shift ... which is a massive barrier. I think that's almost a generational change.

The Managing Partner of a law firm observed,

> If managers say that they are going to put data, information and knowledge management in place, different parts of the organisation react differently. The operational staff say we're already so under pressure, demand exceeds our capacity tenfold, now you just want to create another stick to hit us over the head with. The guys in the middle say that if you create more work, it will create additional activity that will assume effort and they'd rather use that effort to do real work. The guys at the more senior management, upper management, sit there very quietly. They look at this with a lot of suspicion and think they should make sure this thing dies quickly. They find a way of throttling it.

The CIO of a government department suggested that mistakes are not tolerated,

> There has to be a culture that learning and mistakes are good, because that's how people learn. If there is a culture of prosecution – if I'm wrong it's going to be off with my head – data, information, and knowledge will not be managed.

One of the best quotes we have heard is from the Director Information Systems Division for a defence manufacturer who said,

> We have extraordinary Intellectual Property. The Taliban is trying to shoot it down and [our competition] is trying to reverse engineer it. Yet, we have poor data quality and siloed information. But the battlefield is on the inside of this organisation and no-one, least of me, is going to put their head above the parapet to do a difficult, nebulous, enterprise-wide information management initiative because they are just going to get their head shot off.

- What leadership does your organisation provide in the management of Information Assets? How is that manifested?
- What level of support for the good management of Information Assets does your staff believe is being provided?
- How does your organisation maintain a strong culture of continuous improvement in the management of its Information Assets?
- How is that culture manifested? And how does the organisation benefit from this culture?
- How do you measure good Information Asset management behaviours and discourage bad?
- How do you incentivise and reward good Information Asset management practices?

NOTE

1. Evans, N., & Price, J. 2014. Responsibility and Accountability for Information Asset Management (IAM) in Organisations. *Electronic Journal Information Systems Evaluation*, 17(1): 113–121.

9

What Is Required to Govern and Manage Your Information Assets Well?

INTRODUCTION

In Chapter 8 we addressed:

- the role that leadership and management takes in encouraging good Information Asset management behaviour and discouraging bad practices; and
- how to create the corporate discipline required to manage data, information and knowledge as a strategic business asset.

In this chapter we look at governance and management of the organisation's Information Assets.

EXECUTIVE OVERVIEW

Only with appropriate Information Asset governance (management policies and other instruments) will these assets be managed effectively. Those who provide business governance through monitoring and control of the organisation, i.e. the Board and CEO, should make somebody accountable for the governance and management of the Information Assets. This accountable person should be measured and rewarded on the quality of the organisation's Information Assets and should be at the correct level to influence the strategy of the organisation. Information is only an asset if it can be found and used. To find information, you need to know what it is called and where it is stored.

DOI: 10.4324/9781003439141-9

DOMAIN 5: INFORMATION ASSET ENVIRONMENT

The Information Asset environment domain addresses the governance and management of the organisation's Information Assets. This domain applies the principles of the business environment domain to the governance and management of the organisation's Information Assets. The information environment domain addresses the organisation's Information Asset:

- Governance and accountability.
- Management and responsibility.
- Vision, mission, strategy, goals and objectives.
- Inventory, including:
    - o value – the most valuable data, information and knowledge should be included on the organisation's Asset Register; and
    - o vulnerability – the most sensitive and vulnerable, like personal data or key persons, should be included on the organisation's risk register,
- Lifecycle.
- Frameworks and tools, including:
    - o principles;
    - o policy and work instructions;
    - o access, security and privacy; and
    - o lifecycle management.

Only with appropriate Information Asset governance (management policies and other instruments) will these assets be managed effectively.

With committed leadership and management (Domain 4), an effective Information Asset governance and management environment including policies and other instruments will be diligently implemented and adherence with them encouraged, thereby creating an effective Information Asset management environment (Domain 5). With an effective Information Asset management environment (Domain 5), information systems are more likely to be fit for purpose (Domain 6).

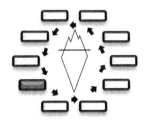

WHAT GOOD AND BAD LOOK LIKE

For the Information Asset environment domain, this is what good and bad look like:

What good looks like	Data, information, content and knowledge are governed as a strategic business asset. Information principles, strategy, policy, guidelines and instruments are effective, maintained and used/adhered to.
What bad looks like	The ownership of, and responsibility for, Information Assets is unclear and defaults to the IT department, whose KPIs are centred on throughput and uptime, not on data quality. The Information Asset management lifecycle and its management are not understood, and instruments including policy and agreed corporate language are neither developed nor implemented.

Throughout this book we have emphasised the importance of governance and management at both business and asset levels. We described the Board and Chief Executive Officer as making the Chief Financial Officer (CFO) accountable for the governance and management of the organisation's Financial Assets. The CFO then governs the asset and delegates authority to those who manage the day-to-day spending and reporting.

It should be precisely the same for the organisation's vital data, information and knowledge, i.e. its Information Assets. Those who provide business governance through monitoring and control of the organisation, i.e. the Board and CEO, should make somebody accountable for the governance and management of the Information Assets. Irrespective of the person's title (let's call them a Chief Information Assets Officer or CIAO) the accountable person should be measured and rewarded on the quality of the organisation's Information Assets. Like the CFO, the CIAO would in turn develop, implement and maintain the instruments by which the Information Assets are managed. The organisation's data, information and knowledge, its Information Assets, are managed by every single person in the organisation. This stipulates that, like the CFO, the CIAO has the raw power and authority to impose Information Asset standards and behaviours upon the entire organisation. Without that authority, the rest of the executive team will simply tell him/her to go and boil their head.

Many organisations have a Chief Information Officer (CIO). In most of those organisations the title is a misnomer. Most CIOs are actually IT Managers or Chief Technology Officers (CTOs). In a few organisations the

CIO is measured on and held accountable for the quality of the organisation's Information Assets. Few organisations have someone who will be sacked if the quality of their Information Assets does not meet predetermined standards.

THE ROLE OF THE CIO

Current thinking about the accountability for Information Assets is still nascent. That new and particularly interesting tool, ChatGPT, scours the internet for information. As on 24th April 2023, this is what it says in response to the question, "What are Information Assets and who is accountable for them?"

> Information assets are any form of data, knowledge, or information that an organisation owns, creates, or uses in its operations. Examples of information assets include financial records, customer data, intellectual property, employee information, and trade secrets. These assets can be stored in a variety of formats, including digital files, paper documents, and other physical media.

Good answer. It goes on.

> Accountability for information assets ultimately falls on the organisation's leadership, particularly the CEO and board of directors.

Another good answer. However, this is where it begins to go pear-shaped.

> However, specific responsibilities for managing information assets may be delegated to other individuals or departments within the organisation, such as the chief information officer (CIO), chief security officer (CSO), or data governance team.

Why is that pear-shaped? Because here's what ChatGPT has to say about the Chief Information Officer.

> The CIO is responsible for the overall technology strategy of the organisation, including managing and implementing the technology infrastructure, applications, and services that support the business. The CIO is typically focused on the operational aspects of technology and ensuring that it meets the needs

of the business. They are also responsible for managing the IT department, including hiring and training staff, setting budgets, and ensuring that the department is aligned with the overall goals of the organisation.

This finding is corroborated by a March 2023 survey of consulting engineering firms that reveals:

- AECOM's CIO "leads Information Technology (IT) for the enterprise and is responsible for the development and execution of the global IT strategy, including overseeing its infrastructure and operations".
- Arup's CIO leads "Arup's strategic digital technology ambitions globally, bringing over 20 years of experience of technology and digital leadership, digital content development, cloud capabilities and strategic cyber security practice".
- GHD's CIO "is an executive leader responsible for technology and technical applications".

It is further corroborated by our research findings. The Chief Knowledge Officer of a pipeline operator, said,

> The CIO wasn't interested. It wasn't an issue to him. Nobody had come to him and said you need to get information in order. His focus was on the technology element. For him, his biggest issue was speed and access. That's what he focused on. Not actually the managing of the information and the content. There was nobody that would take ownership.

So, the current thinking is that accountability for Information Assets should be delegated to:

- a Chief Information Officer (CIO) who looks after the technology;
- a Chief Security Officer (CSO) who is not responsible for the quality of the organisation's Information Asset or for leveraging and exploiting them; or
- a data governance team whose remit is limited to just data and governance, i.e. policy.

It's not good enough. We are still not thinking about managing our data, information and knowledge as the vital and strategic business asset it is.

Our research has indicated that few organisations understand what information drives their business and they lack good information asset governance and management that support the organisation's goals.

A CFO commented,

> We have not done a good job yet of defining what is our core business. If we can't define our core business, it's difficult to define what information is valuable to it.

The person who is supposedly accountable for the management of Information Assets is often not at the correct level to influence the strategy of the organisation; they are rarely on the executive level where their voice will be heard. In one of the organisations that was surveyed in our research, a pipeline operator, the Records Manager was responsible for the management of data, information and knowledge, but the Chief Knowledge Officer commented that the Records Manager was not at the right level in the organisation to be heard,

> He was making noise, but he wasn't getting anywhere.

She added:

> When I came on board, I started regular meetings and communication. I had a group role as CKO, whereas he did not.

WHAT IS REQUIRED TO GOVERN AND MANAGE YOUR INFORMATION ASSETS WELL?

We mentioned in Chapter 2 that Information is only an asset if it can be found and used. If not, it instantly becomes a liability. To find information, you need to know only two things – what it's been called and where it's been stored or saved. Naming a piece of information appropriately and saving it in the correct place requires corporate discipline and incentive. To ensure appropriate naming and correct storage, a file plan and naming conventions can be used. These are cheap and effective. More sophistication adds metadata and enterprise search. More sophistication again adds natural language processing, artificial intelligence and other high-end tools.

There is no point in keeping and managing everything; most of the information in our organisations is rubbish (it's not relevant, accurate, correct, fit for purpose, complete, etc.) and to keep it would constitute an unwarranted waste of valuable resources. It is thus an Information Liability and should be thrown out. We need to know what to keep and manage – and we need to know what to get rid of. Some information is highly valuable and sensitive. It needs to be cared for and protected. The right information needs to be provided to the right people at the right time. It must not be provided to the right people at the wrong time or the wrong people at the right time.

The following is required for effective governance and management of the Information Assets:

- A clear understanding of the business and precisely what it does. This could take the form of an Activities Map, Business Classification Scheme, a Capability Map and/or process maps. Intimately understanding the business enables clarity around the allocation and deployment of scarce resources.
- Clearly defined language of the business. This could take the form of an enterprise thesaurus or glossary or simply preferred and non-preferred terms. One university has four different definitions of the term "student commencement". How can you run a business like that?
- A clear understanding of the Information Assets used to conduct the business activities of the organisation. This could take the form of an Information Asset Inventory or an Information Value and Performance Map.
- A clear understanding of the business impact of the Information Assets – the risk, cost, value, benefit and ethical implications to the organisation. This should extend to understanding the value of Information Assets to each part of the business and of their sensitivity and how they should be protected.
- Awareness by the senior executive of the importance of Information Assets to the business and willingness to govern and manage them well.
- Accountability imposed for the management of the organisation's Information Assets.
- The leadership and management instruments required to set, maintain, measure and encourage a culture of valuing data, information and knowledge as a vital business asset;
- Information Asset management strategy, policy and procedures.
- Fundamental, immutable guiding principles.
- A framework or structure enabling a single system of record and a single source of truth. The CFO doesn't record expenditure in multiple places and, similarly, information must not be kept in multiple places. A simple analogy is if you give somebody a watch then (s)he can tell the time. If you give them two watches then they will never, ever know which one is correct.

- An ability to find the information required. As mentioned above, this can be enabled through a simple file plan and naming conventions through to high-end tools. But there is a prerequisite. By itself, no software can do the job; human judgement is required.
- Management of the lifecycle of the organisation's Information Assets including destroying them at the end of their life.
- Measurement of the quality of the organisation's Information Assets.
- Measurement of the benefits enjoyed by staff and the organisation from having high-quality Information Assets.

- In what ways does your organisation govern and manage its Information Assets with the same levels of governance, discipline and rigour as that with which it manages its Financial Assets?
- What would your organisation look like if it managed its money the way it manages its information?
- If your organisation does not govern and manage its Information Assets the way it should or could, what are the reasons for that?
- Who is responsible for managing the organisation's Information Assets? How is that responsibility articulated?
- Does your organisation have a clear Information Asset vision, principles, strategy, policy and management system? Are those instruments implemented? If not, why not?
- Does your organisation know who creates, captures and uses what Information Assets for what purpose?
- How do you measure the management of your Information Assets? How do you incentivise good Information Asset management practices?
- What instruments does your organisation use to manage its Information Assets?
- Does your organisation know how, and have the capability, to put its Information Assets to work?
- Does your organisation have the capacity and ability to do the work?

10

What Is the Contribution of Your Information Technology?

INTRODUCTION

In Chapter 9 we discussed the importance of good governance and management of the organisation's Information Assets.

In this chapter we will:

- highlight the role of the Information Technology (IT) team as a critical business partner and enabler;
- caution against asking the IT team to do things that they are not measured on, not paid to do and are simply incapable of doing; and
- show how intuitive, easy-to-use IT encourages and supports good Information Asset behaviour.

EXECUTIVE OVERVIEW

Information Technology and Information Asset management are completely different and they should never be confused. In many cases, it is assumed that information management means deploying new technology solutions. Structured data are often managed with technology, but unstructured data and knowledge are much more difficult to manage. The CIO/IT Manager must not be held accountable for the quality of the organisation's Information Assets, as (s)he is measured on other KPIs.

DOI: 10.4324/9781003439141-10

DOMAIN 6: INFORMATION TECHNOLOGY

The Information Technology domain represents the technical and physical objects and instruments (hardware, software and telecommunications) required to deliver the right information to the right people at the right time.

For decades now, Information Technology has become increasingly and rapidly more important. It underpins and enables every part of our lives.

With the right Information Asset governance and management (Domain 5), Information Technology is more likely to be used efficiently and effectively (Domain 6). For example, the information environment will stipulate clear language and storage location resulting in a single source of truth/system of record. In turn, usable and fit-for-purpose Information Technology (Domain 6) will support good Information Asset management behaviours (Domain 7).

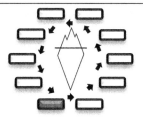

WHAT GOOD AND BAD LOOK LIKE

For the Information Technology domain, this is what good and bad look like:

What good looks like	Information Technology supports rather than hinders good Information Asset management, ensuring a single source of truth (a single version, no duplication) in a single system of record (Finance system, Customer Relationship Management system) that is easily created, saved, found and used.
What bad looks like	Unlike Financial Assets for which the Chart of Accounts stipulates one place and one place only for their management and reporting, Information Assets have multiple, disjointed systems and repositories creating an environment that prevents their effective management. IT systems are slow, cumbersome, not intuitive, poorly explained and taught and the full functionality of the technology is not used. Poor IT systems encourage workarounds and other poor behaviours.

This next point is extremely important. Information Technology and Information Asset management are two sides of the same coin. They have a symbiotic relationship and need one another in order to maximise their efficiency and effectiveness. Nothing that we say in this chapter in any way diminishes the vital importance of IT and nothing that we say contains any criticism, actual or implied, about IT.

When information systems are difficult to use, cumbersome and slow, if technologies malfunction or when requested information is not readily available, people will use the system sub-optimally or not at all, i.e. they will create workarounds. Such workarounds mean that people bypass or undermine the mandated information management practices. Sometimes workarounds are viewed as harmless and essential for performing everyday work. However, poor behaviours often result in inefficiencies, duplication, errors and increased risk, as well as hazardous, unethical or illegal violations of procedures and responsibilities.[1] This view is corroborated by the findings of our research.

A Chief Financial Officer (CFO) said, "IT people talk about [technology] with levels of certainty that are unjustified. They're like the Mercedes salesman who basically says: You'll never have a problem. Well, it's just [nonsense], eventually you will".

A Knowledge Manager commented on the restrictions of technology in their firm:

> Our biggest challenge is the size of our documents. A lot of our design intelligence is image based. We can have files that could be as large as a hundred megabytes.

The Manager of an HR recruitment company said:

> We have a database system that does not really work, as well as inadequate software. It's clunky, it's slow, it's excessively manual in its data input and so forth. We can visualise a system that would be better, but we don't know quite where to find it. It's hard to buy stuff that you don't know much about because you're worried that you're going to make a mistake. Business owners are worried about spending a lot of money on something that might actually be worse than what they've got because you hear stories of people doing just that.

Information Technology and Information Asset management are completely different, and they should never be confused. It is often wrongly assumed that information is synonymous with Information Technology. Robertson (2005) says that, in many cases, "information management" has meant deploying new technology solutions, such as content or document management systems, data warehousing or portal applications. Logan (2010) agrees that the Information Technology function owns the systems that are used to create and store Information Assets. Their job is to manage information technology, the hardware, software and networks. The business people who produce and use the information inherently know its value and understand what contribution it makes to their part of the business. However, it is often difficult to get business people to articulate their information needs. They do not wish to waste their valuable time performing Information Asset management tasks. In Logan's words,

> And so the circular argument begins: it is not my job, IT should do it, by which they mean buy more storage and get us that piece of magic software that will fix the problem once and for all.[2]

So how do we handle this? We handle it by deliberately and consciously separating Information Technology from Information Assets. Information Technology is the delivery mechanism. Information Assets are the data, information and knowledge; they are the content that gets delivered. Think of a glass of wine.

   Information Technology is the glass – the delivery mechanism. Information Assets are the content – the wine. The purpose of the technology is to provide the delivery mechanism for the content. Consider this analogy: When you order a delicious South Australian Barossa Valley Shiraz at a restaurant, does the sommelier pour it into your hands? No, it's presented to you in a fine and graceful wine glass. The content is the wine, and the delivery mechanism is the glass. They are different things, they have different purposes. The value lies in the wine – that's what you actually pay for. You don't pay for the glass, which goes back to the kitchen to be washed and served to the next customer. The glass may be beautiful and elegant, but if the wine is vinegar, you won't have a great experience.

When he explains the difference between delivery technology and content, Tom Redman uses the analogy of the movie industry. When Tom and I were little boys, to see a movie we had to go to a cinema. You watched the movie of your choice at the time of your choice in the place of your choice. Then the development of the video tape recorder changed all that. You could hire a movie of your choice and play it at the time of your choice in the comfort of your own home. Now we can stream movies and watch them whenever we want, wherever we are on whatever device we like. The technology is fantastic. But it doesn't stop a rubbish movie from being rubbish.

These days, when we have an information problem, we give that problem to the people with "Information" in their name to solve. What do Information Technology professionals do? They do what they are measured on and paid to do. They buy a tool to fix the problem. So, let's think about this. When we have a financial problem, for instance a cash flow issue from overdue payments, what do we do? Do we rush out and buy some accounting software? No. We ring up our clients and ask them to pay their bills. So why on earth do we rush out and buy software when we have an information problem? There are two issues with this.

Firstly, the business, take for instance the Chief Legal Counsel, knows more about what (s)he does, in this case the practice of law, than the IT department does. (S)he knows more about what data, information and knowledge is required to practise law than IT does, and (s)he is more interested in the quality of those Information Assets than IT experts are. Data, information and knowledge are not an IT asset. IT practitioners do not use the business' information, they do not understand it, they cannot manage it and they cannot be held responsible for it.

Secondly, IT function is measured on throughput, uptime, cost minimisation and perhaps usability, not on information quality. IT professionals are terrific at planning, designing, developing, selecting, procuring, installing, implementing and maintaining the IT infrastructure that delivers to the organisation the vital data, information and content it needs to perform its business. That is their job. The people in IT are smart, professional and helpful, but it is utterly unfair to ask them to take responsibility for the quality of an organisation's Information Assets. The executive who asks them to do that is setting IT up for failure.

Danette McGilvray presents it like this:

A hammer does not make you a carpenter, but you cannot be a good carpenter without a hammer.

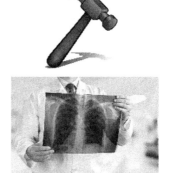

Thinking the right tool will take care of all your data quality problems is like believing the right x-ray machine will make you healthy

The tools can only do so much. Structured data are often managed with technology, but unstructured data and knowledge are difficult to manage. A CIO from the Australian Health industry commented:

> Unstructured information is difficult to manage. There are some clever engines [...] but I've never really seen anything that produces much of use. It always comes back to the fact that information that's not captured in a structured format becomes very difficult to manage. So, the technology has not been particularly effective.

Information Technology and Information Management (indeed all asset classes) must not be confused; they have or require different approaches as indicated in Table 10.1.

If that's the case, why on earth would you ~~abdicate~~ give the responsibility for the management of the organisation's most valuable asset to IT? Another representation is shown in Table 10.2.

What we are trying to highlight is the intellectual chasm between intangible and physical assets, and between Information Assets and the technology that delivers them.

TABLE 10.1

Information Assets vs Information Technology

	Information Assets	**Information Technology**
Accountability	Very few organisations hold an individual accountable for the quality of its Information Assets.	IT Manager. The IT Manager can be held accountable for the IT infrastructure in, e.g. an oil and gas company, but (s)he cannot be held accountable for the quality of the seismic data.
Ownership	The owner of the organisation's Information Assets will typically be that department for which those assets create the most value. For instance, the finance team will own the organisation's financial information and the geophysicists will own the organisation's seismic information.	IT Manager. Typically, the IT department owns the servers, routers and software. The business, e.g. the Exploration department in an oil and gas company, owns the seismic data, information and content that the business generates and analyses.
Responsibility	Every single person in an organisation is responsible for managing its Information Assets well.	IT Department. Typically, the IT department has responsibility for the servers, routers and software. IT staff can be held responsible for the uptime and throughput of the computer network, but they cannot maintain the seismic data or be held responsible for knowing the size of the organisation's oil and gas reserves.
Instruments	The organisation should have a single person responsible for the instruments that help manage the organisation's Information Assets. These instruments can include a Business Classification Scheme, Information Asset Inventory, Thesaurus, Information Asset Value Model, Security Model, Metadata Model, Master and Reference Data Models and Retention and Disposal Schedule.	The IT Manager is responsible for the instruments that help manage the organisation's IT infrastructure. The IT team can implement and use instruments that show network performance, manage maintenance schedules or monitor software licences, but it doesn't know how to build the instruments required to manage an Information Asset framework, language or lifecycle.

(Continued)

TABLE 10.1 (CONTINUED)

Information Assets vs Information Technology

	Information Assets	**Information Technology**
Behaviours	Leadership and management are responsible for the Information Asset behaviours of staff.	The IT Manager is responsible for the behaviour of the IT Department. The IT department can create an enterprise IT environment and prevent the proliferation of unsanctioned (feral) systems, but it cannot set the required Information Asset management expectations and incentives to ensure high-quality data.
Measurement	Information Asset quality.	Throughput, uptime, cost management and perhaps usability. IT can measure the effectiveness of the infrastructure, but cannot measure the quality of the data.
Justification and funding	I have never seen an organisation that continually invests in the quality of its Information Assets based on the business benefits that accrue from managing them well.	IT infrastructure project business cases. IT professionals can justify the purchase of IT infrastructure, but it cannot identify the risks, costs, value, benefits and ethics associated with the management of the organisation's Information Assets and the justification of the investment required for continuous data quality improvement.
Costs	What is the cost of creating, acquiring, using and managing the organisation's Information Assets?	The cost of hardware, software, upgrades, maintenance, support, telecommunications and IT staff salaries.
Value	What is the value of the organisation's Information Assets?	IT infrastructure is a rapidly depreciating asset.
Benefits	How are the benefits of managing the organisation's Information Assets well measured?	As identified in the IT infrastructure project business cases.

(*Source:* Experience Matters)

TABLE 10.2

Business' Interests vs IT's Interests

	Business' Interests	**IT department's Interests**
Their objective	Business results Managed risk Competitive advantage Cost effectiveness	99% uptime Throughput Mobility, web Cost minimisation
Their job	Good business decisions Products and services Maximum client value	Planning Design Procurement Installation Maintenance Support

What they need	Business knowledge
	Resources
	  • Financial Assets/annual budget
	  • Physical Assets/property and
	    infrastructure including IT
	  • Human Assets/people
	  • Information Assets/data, information
	    and knowledge
	Right information to the right people at the
	right time
		Hardware
		Applications
		Telecommunications
		IT staff

The outcome	Information quality	Infrastructure and delivery quality

(*Source:* Experience Matters)

- What is the role of Information Technology (IT)?
- Upon what is IT measured?
- How is the CIO/IT Manager measured and incentivised?
- How can the CIO/IT Manager be held truly accountable for the quality of the organisation's Information Assets?

NOTES

1. Alter, Steven. 2014. *Theory of Workarounds. Communications of the Association for Information Systems.* 34. 10.17705/1CAIS.03455.
2. Logan, D. 2010. What Is Information Governance and Why Is It So Hard? Gartner Blog. Available at: http://blogs.gartner.com/debra_logan/2010/01/11/what-is-information-governance-and-why-is-it-so-hard/.

11

What Is the Impact of Behaviour on the Way Information Assets Are Managed?

INTRODUCTION

In Chapter 10 we:

- highlighted the role of the Information Technology (IT) team as a critical business partner and enabler;
- cautioned against asking the IT team to do things that they are not measured on, not paid to do and are simply incapable of doing; and
- showed how intuitive, easy-to-use IT encourages and supports good Information Asset behaviour.

In this chapter we will discuss:

- the impact of organisational politics and human behaviour on the information culture of the organisation;
- Information Asset ownership behaviours; and
- Information Asset sharing behaviours, including
  - o information hoarding that leads to information landfill, and
  - o information hiding that leads to information bunkers.

EXECUTIVE OVERVIEW

Human behaviour has fascinated, puzzled and challenged organisations for many decades. This is even more true in the digital age. Information

DOI: 10.4324/9781003439141-11

behaviour refers to the way people within the organisation work with and manage data, information and knowledge. The culture of an organisation significantly influences how well these Information Assets are managed by individuals. Many organisations' Information Asset management culture does not reflect good practice. As we found through our research, most of the barriers to the effective management of Information Assets relate to attitudes and behaviour displayed by leaders and employees.

Such human-behavioural barriers include a lack of interest; inefficient communication between stakeholders; lack of culture of information and knowledge sharing; lack of competence of staff; and lack of incentives. Changing these attitudes and addressing the behaviour is crucial because organisations rarely face a single existential challenge; rather, the attitudes and resulting poor information behaviour lead to a slow commercial "death by a thousand cuts" (Evans & Price, 2018). For example, managing a single e-mail ineffectively is insignificant to company performance, whereas every person managing every e-mail poorly every day has a negative productivity impact that could represent an existential threat to the organisation.

DOMAIN 7: INFORMATION ASSET BEHAVIOUR

The Information Asset management behaviour domain refers to the way people within the organisation work with and manage information.[1,2]

Efficient and effective information systems (Domain 6) support good information management behaviours (Domain 7). If systems are difficult to use, people will use them sub-optimally, create workarounds or not use them at all. Good Information Asset management behaviours create high-quality Information Assets (Domain 8).

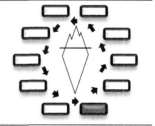

WHAT GOOD AND BAD LOOK LIKE

For the Information Asset behaviour domain, this is what good and bad look like:

What good looks like	Staff understand the benefit of high-quality data, information, content and knowledge to both themselves and the organisation, and willingly adhere to corporate Information Asset management policy. They are willing to share data, information and knowledge with colleagues and other stakeholders. And good Information Asset management behaviours such as sharing information and knowledge, complying with rules and regulations, protecting the assets and responsible deletion are encouraged, measured and rewarded.
What bad looks like	Information is often named and stored haphazardly as staff think that their information is a personal possession, not a corporate resource. Information is hoarded as staff don't understand its value to the organisation. Information is also often hidden to prevent it from being found, used, shared and exploited, mostly for political or power purposes.

INFORMATION BEHAVIOUR

In Chapter 3 we identified the barriers to managing Information Assets well. Whatever the causes, they are often manifested in the Information Asset management behaviours of the organisation's staff. Amongst many causes we have identified:

- a lack of executive interest;
- a lack of governance at the business level in which an accountable person imposes Information Asset management standards and behaviour on the organisation;
- a lack of leadership in creating expectation setting, encouragement, measurement and incentivisation;
- a lack of induction, education and training; and
- clunky, hard-to-use IT systems.

The Chief Information Officer (CIO) of a County government department pointed out that maintaining high-quality data and information is too difficult, so staff avoid doing it.

Whilst information management policies have been endorsed by the county's chief administrative officer, people will find workarounds if they do not like the system. Further, people are prone to store information in their own environments. There is no compulsion to use the system and the county attorney's office relies on individuals' professionalism to ensure that it is used.

The Managing Partner of a law firm observed that people are afraid of being exposed and "when you're pointing inefficiencies out to people, most will resist". He added, "our organisation is slightly schizophrenic in that there's a group who want to see an investment in information and a group that feels very threatened by information".

People regard information as power and therefore they are protecting their interests as it gives them a position of power. Hoarding information provides protection against job loss. People also consider company information as their own property and store it on their own hard drives. The Chief Knowledge Officer (CKO) of a State government agency added that people don't trust the information systems and therefore they are sceptical, so they store their information physically two or three times:

> You're actually saying, I'm going to wrestle these filing drawers out from under your desk and put it in a system that everyone can see, and you get enough people that are horrified by that, and you don't get the "yes moment" to go ahead and do it. Because you just get bogged down in the organisation.

People are basically selfish, and the Chief Financial Officer (CFO) of a Rail utilities company commented, "the direction of the organisation is nothing to do with the direction of the individuals".

OWNERSHIP OF INFORMATION ASSETS

The "psychological ownership theory" (Pierce, Kostova and Dirks, 2003) is a well-known principle that states that people who have control over an object eventually have feelings of ownership of that object – *I am what I have*. Given that data, information and knowledge are acquired, controlled or created by individuals, people may regard them as their personal property. People have a mindset of "I produced or contributed to it and therefore it is mine and only mine". This attitude contributes to the following Information Asset management behaviours.

INFORMATION SHARING BEHAVIOURS

Information sharing behaviour is an important aspect of organisational commitment to information management. The information sharing culture of an organisation and the behaviour of its staff significantly influence how well its information is managed. Negative information management behaviour that results from misplaced ownership can be categorised into two types: (i) unintentional hoarding and (ii) intentional hiding.

Information Hoarding

Information hoarding means that accumulated enterprise information such as e-mails, documents and numerous other file types are stored haphazardly on a variety of servers, hard drives and flash disks. Such hoarding results when people regard enterprise data, information and knowledge as low-value assets that do not need to be stored safely and shared with others. Danette McGilvray observes that information hoarding also happens when people know the value of the information but do not trust the systems and processes that store and share the information. They hoard it because they think no one else is taking care of it. As a result, important information remains with individuals and valuable and irreplaceable items are stored in a public area with an increased likelihood that it may leak into the wrong hands or simply be lost. Some staff insist that all information should be saved forever, as one never knows when it might be needed. Information hoarding results in "digital landfill". The bigger the landfill, the more information must be inspected to find an important document, e-mail or file.

The Chief Financial Officer of an automotive services company commented that

> We are a classic siloed organisation with limited sharing of information between departments. This situation is currently changing. We're now recognising that we need to do that now in a better way, and we are creating our library and bringing the business together and sharing information a lot more than what we ever did.

A Knowledge Manager in Australia confirmed that "[*information sharing*] requires a culture shift, which is a massive barrier; I think that's almost a generational change". The CKO of an Australian government department admitted that information is kept in various places on various servers in the agency and even stored on old servers that have been archived:

> It is stored electronically, in hard copy, in different physical places and accessed by different computers on the site; it can't be shared, it can't be found. This is a massive challenge for our organisation, "because we've got buckets of information everywhere; we've got Access databases all over the place; we've got people with 20 years" worth of work stuck in an e-mail box or on a disk, with masses of information in their personal drives, just because they've never been told not to put their information there.

The Managing Partner of a law firm commented,

> I encourage people that whenever they produce any document or give any advice that is unique to send it to our library people for inclusion either in precedents or in the opinions register. The problem with that is, not everyone thinks to do it… because you're busy.

The Chair of the Board of a large, successful law firm said,

> The secretary stores the document she changed for me on her own hard drive. She just doesn't think about other people needing it. If something happens to her it will be a bit of a challenge to find it as everyone saves information in their own way.

Information Hiding

Hiding refers to behaviours where data, information and knowledge are purposefully withheld from co-workers, i.e. it is "fortified and defended". Internal politics are sometimes more important than the overall organisation and employees therefore often use withholding information as a weapon. They keep specifically requested information and knowledge from another person through:

- evasive conduct – providing useless information to the information requester;

- playing dumb – pretending to know nothing about the information that is requested; and
- rationalised hiding – claiming that they lack authorisation to provide the requested information.[3]

Hiding behaviour is malicious, often due to fear of being exposed to inadequate or incorrect information, organisational politics and power needs. It is also based on fear of information misuse, mistrust and loss of job security. Information hiding results in "bunker information" that is impossible to access.

An example of purposeful hiding occurs in the legal industry, where the success of a partner in a law firm is based on the number of cases they attract and win. These practitioners often over-value information and this makes them hesitant to share knowledge and risk losing their competitive edge. The lawyers protect their access to clients even if colleagues request the information.

People often work for their own personal advantage rather than the good of the organisation. They are selfish and manage their own interests. A participant in our research commented,

> There are many "what's in it for me people out there" and that "most people in organisations are only focused on survival and have their own agendas. They do not make the best decisions for the business; it's all about their own agenda".

Hiding information therefore provides protection against job loss.

RESISTANCE TO INFORMATION ASSET MANAGEMENT PROGRAMMES

People often resist the implementation of an Information Asset management programme. The reasons for such resistance include loss of identity, changes to the familiar environment, loss of power and influence, individual personality differences, inability to understand the benefits of the change, lack of discipline, time pressure and a feeling of being overloaded with responsibilities. Resistance to proper Information Asset management leads to employees openly expressing negative emotions, reverting to old ways of doing things and bargaining to be exempted from new policies or processes. These in turn lead to a reduction in productivity and efficiency, increased cost and missed deadlines. Managers might also resist the change by refusing or being reluctant to provide the resources required to implement a planned Information Asset management programme, by cancelling or refusing to attend critical meetings and through a lack of sponsorship and endorsement of the programme.

EVERYBODY'S RESPONSIBILITY

Tom Redman advocates that staff have a responsibility to create awareness about the importance of data, information and knowledge. He creates a scenario in which Stephanie, an aspiring executive, is about to present to the Board of her organisation. One of her staff comes in and tells her that the data from the Widget Department is incorrect; this is of substantial concern for her presentation and perhaps her career. Happily, within the hour, her staff member comes in again and tells Stephanie that the problem has been found, the data corrected and the presentation updated. The presentation is an unqualified success, and everybody is happy.

But are they? Stephanie has not done the boss of the Widget Department the courtesy of telling him that his data is incorrect. That is the data equivalent of leaving a dropped banana skin on the floor of a busy corridor which, in some organisations with a strong culture of human safety, would be a dismissible offence. The point is that it is incumbent upon every member of staff to take responsibility for managing their data, information and knowledge.

- How would you describe good and bad Information Asset management behaviours?
- What questions do you ask about the way managers and staff manage data, information and knowledge?

NOTES

1. Evans, N., & Price, J. 2018. Death by a Thousand Cuts: Information Asset Management Attitudes and Behaviours practices in organisations. *Information Research,* 23(1): 779.
2. Evans, N., & Price, J. 2017. Managing Information in Law Firms: Changes and Challenges. *Information Research,* 22(1).
3. Kang, S. W. (2016). Knowledge Withholding: Psychological Hindrance to the Innovation Diffusion within an Organisation. *Knowledge Management Research and Practice (KMRP):* 144–149.

12

What Is Information Asset Quality and Why Is It So Important?

INTRODUCTION

In Chapter 11 we discussed:

- the impact of organisational politics and human behaviour on the information culture of the organisation;
- Information Asset ownership behaviours; and
- Information Asset sharing behaviours including
  - information hoarding that leads to information landfill, and
  - information hiding that leads to information bunkers.

In this chapter we will describe and explain:

- the attributes of data and information;
- what good and bad quality Information Assets look like;
- why high-quality Information Assets are so important;
- how to measure the quality of Information Assets;
- the causes of poor Information Asset management and how to maximise the probability of success;
- how to create, improve, manage and sustain Information Asset quality; and
- how executives can make a difference and what they need to know about Information Asset quality.

DOI: 10.4324/9781003439141-12

EXECUTIVE OVERVIEW

High-quality data are needed to support decision-making and contribute to competitive advantage. However, organisations often work with poor-quality data, information and knowledge. If software is using poor-quality data, then poor-quality data is simply presented more quickly. Everybody in the organisation needs to be good at being both a data creator and customer. Executives must understand *why* having high-quality Information Assets is important, *what* to do and *how* to do it. This requires resources, accountability and committed leadership.

DOMAIN 8: INFORMATION ASSET QUALITY

The Information Asset quality domain addresses the quality of the Information Assets in terms of:

- availability (can it be found in a timely manner?);
- correctness (does it match what it is supposed to be?);
- completeness (is information missing?);
- currency (is it outdated for the intended purpose?); and
- relevance or applicability (is it fit for intended purpose and usefully supports employee research, decision-making and action?).

Good Information Asset management behaviours (Domain 7) create high-quality Information Assets (Domain 8). High-quality information allows these Information Assets to be effectively exploited and leveraged (Domain 9).

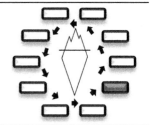

Alan Duncan, an analyst at Gartner,[1] told us a great story. At a Board meeting, when approval was being sought for a proposed data strategy, delivery roadmap and business case, the Executive Vice President and Head of Retail Banking of Middle Eastern bank said, "Data is like a public lavatory; everybody wants to use it, but nobody wants to clean it". Brilliant. Approval was unanimous. In the same Board meeting, in reference to governance and accountability, the same executive said, "We must allow [the Head of Information Management] to draw his sword", a very Middle Eastern metaphor for the level of delegated authority and trust they were agreeing to invest in that person.

In Chapter 2 we mentioned that the term "garbage in, garbage out" has been around since 1864 and is still just as, if not more, relevant today. Yet, we seem to have learned nothing since then. There is a lot of excitement about flash technologies – artificial intelligence, block chain, business intelligence, digital twins and machine learning. But it is all irrelevant if the data the technology is using is rubbish.

We hear plenty of organisations saying, "We want to drive business outcomes and to get those outcomes we need technology". We hear very few organisations saying, "We want to drive business outcomes and to get those outcomes we need the right information".

WHAT GOOD AND BAD LOOK LIKE

For the Information Asset quality domain, this is what good and bad look like:

What good looks like	Information Assets are: • available and timely (can be found quickly/in a timely manner); • accurate/correct (it matches what it is supposed to be); • complete (information is not missing); • current (it is not outdated for the intended purpose); and • relevant (it is fit for intended purpose and usefully supports decision-making and action).
What bad looks like	Data quality is around 65%–70%, resulting in bad decisions, mistakes, poor productivity and waste. Information Asset quality is not ensured at the point of creation or capture. Management gets excited about modern technology without understanding that it cannot be effective with poor-quality data – garbage in, garbage out. Risk is high and productivity is low. Staff are frustrated and morale is poor.

WHAT HIGH-QUALITY INFORMATION ASSETS INVOLVES

The findings from our research and anecdotal evidence show that:

- organisations' data, information and knowledge are often of poor quality;
- high-quality data are needed to support decision-making and contribute to competitive advantage; and
- if software is using poor-quality data, then poor-quality data is simply presented more quickly.

In Tom Redman's prolific experience, most data are in far worse shape than most people believe … only 3% of companies' data meets basic quality requirements".[2]

He tells us:

1. Almost every data quality situation involves two aspects:
   - is the data right; and
   - is it the right data?
2. The quality of the data is dependent upon context, namely:
   - *is it the right data* depends on what the data is being used for; and
   - *is the data right* is important because sometimes "to the nearest million dollars" is good enough and sometimes pennies matter?
3. There may be many other aspects to data quality, depending on the situation. For example:
   - In many situations a set of data that is "complete" with respect to the task at hand is important (managers should ask, "Is this the full story?").
   - In training artificial intelligence models, bias in training data leads to biased models, (so ask, "are there biases hidden in the training set?").
   - Some decisions are time-sensitive, so it is important that the data be current (so ask, "is this the latest?").
   - Is the data fit for use?

In summary, is the data fit for use, in this context, by that person, at that time?"[3]

Tom describes a great scenario to illustrate the point about "is the data right?" and "is this the right data?" in which you receive a phone call from the principal of your child's school telling you that your child has been suspended for fighting. When you see your child and you ask him/her, "How was your day?" They reply, "It was great, Dad, I achieved an A in my Maths test." In this case the information he/she provided is clearly correct, your child did indeed achieve an A for Maths. But it is not the right information; it is not the information you wanted to hear. The complete information would be "Dad, I achieved an A for my maths test, but I also got suspended".

Context, i.e. the situation at hand, will influence the quality of the information. And the quality of the information will influence the value of the information. In this case, perhaps a different question could have elicited the more complete answer mentioned above, e.g. "Can you tell me about both the good and bad things that happened to you at school today?" The more complete answer would have provided higher quality information. And higher quality information would have delivered more value, certainly to you as the parent.

When we think about Information Asset quality, we start by thinking about who the client is (could be internal or external) and what the client wants to do. Is this information fit for use in this context by this person at this time? Is it the right information and is the information right? This is compounded by the proliferation of Artificial Intelligence (AI). For AI to really work, it needs unbiased, high-quality data and a lot of it.

WHY DATA QUALITY IS SO IMPORTANT

Why is high-quality data so important? Further to what we described in Chapter 5, Tom identifies the business impacts from the way Information Assets are managed. He says, "Bad data is like a virus; you never know where or when it will turn up and what damage it will do. And in times of crisis, good data matters more than ever. Good data is such an accelerant and bad data just creates friction". These business impacts include the following.

- **Time wasted correcting errors.** Tom's evidence is that around "50% of a person's time is wasted dealing with mundane data issues". Remember that this does not include the opportunity cost of not doing the work that should have been done.

- **Mistakes.** Even though people try to correct errors, mistakes leak through to customers, reports and decisions.
- **Lack of trust.** According to a Harvard Business Review survey, only 16% of managers trust the data they use every day. In Tom's words, "Life depends upon trust, and I don't see how you can do anything without it". Interestingly, if 16% of managers trust their data, then either the data quality of their organisations is 84%, which is unlikely, or a significant number of managers erroneously trust incorrect data. But, it gets worse. Customer data is used by marketing, sales, the delivery team, accounts receivable and other parts of the business. So, if the customer data is wrong, the pain inflicted by that poor-quality data is replicated throughout the entire organisation.
- **Revenue wastage.** At company level, the best estimate is that 20% of revenue is wasted due to bad data.
- **Disasters play out in public.** Great examples include Boeing's 737 Max disaster and Rio Tinto's destruction of the Juukan Caves. In the Boeing case, the 737 Max was grounded worldwide after 346 people died in two crashes caused by erroneous angle of attack data. In the Rio Tinto case, in May 2020, Rio Tinto permanently destroyed the Juukan Caves. Michael L'Estrange reported that the destruction of the caves was due to "a series of flaws in [Rio Tinto's] systems, sharing of information, engaging with the Indigenous people and decision-making". The fallout was disastrous. The Chair, CEO, Head of Iron Ore and Head of Corporate Affairs all lost their jobs. But worse was the damage to Rio Tinto's corporate reputation and social licence to operate. And worst of all was the loss of the only inland site in Australia with evidence of continuous human occupation for over 46,000 years, including through the last Ice Age. As Pat Dodson said, "The destruction of these ancient sites was a disaster for our nation and the world".
- **Cost blowouts.** At country level, in 2016 IBM produced a report that estimated that bad data costs the economy of the USA $3.1 trillion per year.[4]
- **Dissatisfaction.** Whether they are internal or external to the organisation, people affected by bad quality or compromised data become angry – and the cost of that is difficult to calculate. Yesterday, as I write this, it was reported that a data breach has cost Australia's second largest telecommunications provider, 10% of its mobile customers and "56 per cent of current customers are considering changing telcos". The breach was enabled by IT people

using real client data in a poorly protected software test environment. One wonders if that practice could have happened if the business and its vital data were properly governed. And this morning I read that a data breach of Australia's largest private health insurer has wiped nearly $2 billion off its market capitalisation.

- **Strategic issues.** It becomes tougher to pursue any strategy if the data upon which you are basing it is poor.
- **People die.** They die through disease, for example Coronavirus and accidents such as aircraft crashes.

Tom's best estimate is that more than half of these negative risks and impacts can be eliminated by improving the quality of your Information Assets. Alternatively, "the biggest opportunity to improve business performance that most organisations have is to reduce data errors, to 'make data problems go away'. It affects virtually everyone". And the people who address the data quality issues in their work or their team or the organisation become empowered.

MEASURING THE QUALITY OF INFORMATION ASSETS

Tom has developed an assessment called the Friday Afternoon Measurement. It is designed to answer the simple question of "Do I need to worry about Information Asset quality?" This is how it works:

Assemble the last 100 transactions of whatever you do and identify the critical elements of those transactions. Your organisation may sign up customers, renew software licences or make sweaters. Get two or three mates who understand the data, work row by row through the 100 transactions, mark the obvious errors in the critical elements and add up the total of imperfect transactions. For instance, if you make sweaters, work out how many of the transactions are the wrong size, the wrong colour, the wrong collar, the wrong price, etc. You will then know if you need to worry about Information Asset quality because you have explicitly linked the quality of your Information Assets with the performance of the business. Tom has asked hundreds of executives what their expectations of data quality are, and the vast majority have answered, "In the high 90s", i.e. more than 90 out of 100 business transactions are expected to be perfect. However, most organisations' quality is in the high 60s or low 70s meaning that fully one-third of business transactions are incorrect in some way. This is therefore completely unacceptable. Have a look at Tom's video of his Friday Afternoon Measurement.[5]

WHO CAN MAKE A DIFFERENCE?

Everyone can make a difference.

Despite the PC being released to the market in 1981, IBM's global supply chain was still based upon the "build to order" manufacturing process that produced customer-specific mainframe and midrange computers. Every month I would place orders for PC software. Every month those orders would not be filled, and the backorders would mount up. They mounted up until the next version of the software was released and all the now useless, superseded stock would arrive. In those days PC software contributed 2% of IBM Australia's revenue and IBM Australia contributed 2% of global revenue. I tracked every order and added up the revenue foregone through lack of supply. It totalled $50 million per year. Based upon that information we were able to develop a business case that resulted in the global manufacturing process and supply chain being changed and improved to handle volume products. So, there I was, one of the most junior staff in the organisation, able to help change the supply chain of the entire organisation. Everyone can make a difference.

WHAT YOU NEED TO KNOW

There is a lot of emphasis in the media and the industry on Artificial Intelligence, Big Data, Business Intelligence, Block Chain, Cyber Security, Data Science, Digital Transformation, Digital Twins and Machine Learning. This is not where organisations need to start. Organisations need to know how good or bad the management of Information Assets is and the business implications of that management. Tom Redman recommends that organisations should not start with Big Data, but with Small Data. Start with and solve specific problems, celebrate the wins, demonstrate success and benefit, and grow organically from there.

Everyone is a data creator, and everyone is a data user. Everyone sends and receives emails. Everyone creates and reads documents and spreadsheets and reports. ***Everybody is responsible.*** In many ways, this is incredibly ordinary. Everybody needs to understand how to be good at being both a data creator and user. This requires corporate discipline. It is not good enough to abandon corporate governance, fail to impose accountability or abdicate responsibility.

As Tom Redman says,

> As simple as these ideas are, they are also revolutionary. It took society generations to accept the idea that the earth is not flat. On the surface it is observably true that you are a data creator and a data customer or user, but the idea that these roles carry responsibility is both obvious and revolutionary. This creates enormous opportunity for staff and executives.

We introduced Danette McGilvray in Chapter 3. She is the author of *Executing Data Quality Projects: Ten Steps to Quality Data and Trusted Information*, 2nd ed. Her Ten Steps methodology offers a structured, yet flexible approach to managing the quality of data within any organisation. It guides leaders and staff as they connect business strategy (answering "why do we care?") to practical steps for implementation (showing "how to" create, improve and sustain data quality). The resultant high-quality data supports whatever is most important to the organisation, protects its Information Assets and helps manage risk.

WHAT EXECUTIVES NEED TO DO

Once executives understand ***why*** having high-quality Information Assets is important, they need to understand ***what*** to do and ***how*** to do it. But, as Danette says, "There is no point in starting from scratch and reinventing the wheel – get help from the experts".

The first questions executives need to ask are:

1. Do your people and machines have the right information available to them at the right time and place to make decisions and take effective action? If the answer is "no", you have a data quality problem.
2. Can you see evidence such as unhappy customers, security breaches, wasted time, poor or delayed decisions, rework, fines, non-compliance with legal requirements, etc.? If the answer is "yes" it is highly likely that poor-quality data is part or all of the problem.

3. What are the most important needs of the business?
4. What data is required to address those business needs?
5. Do we have the "right-level" of data quality to address them?

Always ensure your data work is tied to the organisation's most important business needs: what is necessary to satisfy customers, provide products and services, manage risk, increase business value, implement strategies, achieve goals, address issues, or take advantage of opportunities. Never address data quality for the sake of data quality.

HOW TO CREATE, IMPROVE, MANAGE AND SUSTAIN DATA QUALITY

There are three main things to consider, namely:

1. **Key concepts** that are crucial to understand in order to do data quality work well.
2. **Structuring the data quality project** provides guidance for organising data quality work. Data quality projects can be driven through Agile or any other project management methodology.
3. **the process** to be undertaken which entails putting the key concepts into action with instructions, examples and templates.

Danette has developed the Ten Steps Process, which is illustrated in Figure 12.1.
Details for each of the Ten Steps can be found in her book, *Executing Data Quality Projects: Ten Steps to Quality Data and Trusted Information*™, 2nd ed.

CAUSES OF FAILURE

The causes of failure in data quality include the following.

- Forgetting the human element. Managing Information Assets is done by every person in the organisation. We are all data creators and users.
- Taking a fragmented, rather than an enterprise, approach to data quality. It is not just about data entry, or data cleansing or reporting;

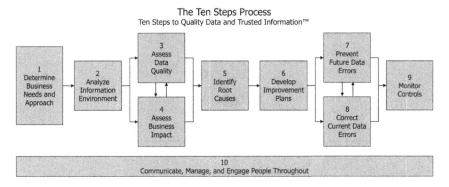

FIGURE 12.1
Ten Steps process. (*Source*: Danette McGilvray)

we need to take an enterprise wide, holistic approach to achieving high-quality data. A holistic approach will address the following:

○ people;
○ organisation;
○ processes;
○ accountability;
○ responsibility;
○ information lifecycle; and
○ technology.

• Failing to realise that technology is a means to an end, not the end in itself, and therefore failing to invest in more than the technology will lead to failure. As Danette says,

> Thinking that technology will improve data quality is like thinking that having an X-ray machine will make me healthy. Of course we need an X-ray machine to use at the right time and place. But we also need doctors, nurses, technicians, and as a patient I have to be motivated to do those things that will improve my health.

HOW TO MAXIMISE THE PROBABILITY OF SUCCESS

To maximise the probability of success in achieving high-quality Information Assets, the executive must be supportive. This must be founded on action; it can't just be lip service that people see straight through. It requires resources, accountability and genuine, committed leadership.

- How do you measure the quality of your Information Assets in terms of:
  - availability/timeliness (can be found quickly/in a timely manner)?;
  - accuracy/correctness (it matches/is what it is supposed to be)?;
  - completeness (information is not missing)?;
  - currency (it is not outdated for the intended purpose)?; and
  - relevance or applicability (it is fit for intended purpose and usefully supports employee research, decision-making and action)?
- How do you incentivise the creation, capture and maintenance of high-quality data, information and knowledge?

NOTES

1. Alan Duncan, 6th March 2023 LinkedIn.
2. https://hbr.org/2017/09/only-3-of-companies-data-meets-basic-quality-standards.
3. Interview with Tom Redman, 3rd February 2022.
4. https://hbr.org/2016/09/bad-data-costs-the-u-s-3-trillion-per-year
5. https://www.youtube.com/watch?v=X8iacfMX1nw.

13

What Is Required to Leverage and Exploit Your Information Assets?

INTRODUCTION

In Chapter 12 we described and explained:

1. the attributes of data and information and show what good and bad quality Information Assets look like;
2. what high-quality Information Assets involves;
3. why high-quality Information Assets are so important;
4. how to measure the quality of Information Assets;
5. the causes of poor Information Asset management and how to maximise the probability of success;
6. how to create, improve, manage and sustain Information Asset quality; and
7. how executives can make a difference and what they need to know about Information Asset quality;

In this chapter we will:

1. build on Chapter 2 to help you understand what your most valuable assets are;
2. discuss why we need to put data, documents, content and knowledge to work to mitigate risk, reduce costs, increase value, drive benefits and ensure ethical corporate behaviour;
3. revisit what is required to establish the foundations from which Information Assets can be leveraged; and
4. show some simple examples of how Information Assets have been put to work with significant, measurable, positive business impact.

DOI: 10.4324/9781003439141-13

EXECUTIVE OVERVIEW

The Information Asset leverage domain considers how an organisation's Information Assets are put to work to identify business opportunities and drive business outcomes. Your organisation can only put Information Assets to work if it knows what the organisation does, how data, information and knowledge are used by the organisation, what information is valuable and sensitive and must therefore be managed, and if it has high-quality information. Executives must understand that if they invest in the management of their Information Assets, they will help mitigate their business risk, see a sizeable return on their investment and make them more competitive by having something no one else does and exploiting it.

DOMAIN 9: INFORMATION ASSET LEVERAGE

The Information Asset leverage domain considers how an organisations' Information Assets are put to work to identify business opportunities and drive business outcomes.

High-quality information (Domain 8) allows Information Assets to be effectively leveraged and exploited (Domain 9). An ability to leverage Information Assets demands the ability to recognise the business impact that ensues (Domain 10).

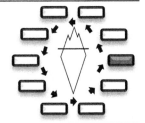

WHAT GOOD AND BAD LOOK LIKE

For the Information Asset leverage domain, this is what good and bad look like:

What good looks like	Information Assets are leveraged to extract the greatest value from the organisation's data, information, content and knowledge and drive the greatest benefit for the organisation.
What bad looks like	The organisation doesn't know what Information Assets it has, or how they can be exploited for business benefit. Opportunities are missed and the organisation's competitive position is compromised.

YOUR MOST VALUABLE ASSETS

What are your most valuable assets? What are your most valuable Information Assets, that is, your most valuable data, information and knowledge? We don't often think about the value of our knowledge, yet we have been including technical knowledge and know-how in our confidentiality and non-disclosure agreements for years. Here's an extract from a typical intellectual property clause in one of those contracts:

> all information of a confidential nature, all information regarding the parties' business interests, all technical knowledge, know-how, unpatented patentable ideas, and all data materials, business records and communications.

What is intellectual property? From the clause above, it is mostly, if not exclusively, Information Assets. Do we manage our intellectual property well? Or do we just slam the trademark and patent certificates in a safe and think we have done enough?

Is corporate knowledge valuable? Is it vulnerable? Here is a couple of anecdotes.

A few years ago, at a Board meeting of a South Australian manufacturing company, the Chair asked the Chief Executive what the organisation's single greatest business risk was. The CEO's answer was that their greatest risk was losing an indispensable staff member called Lewis, as he can access the right information and knowledge at the right time. The Chair responded by ordering the CEO to double Lewis' salary effective the next Monday. Because this would have made Lewis the most highly paid person in the company, the CEO started to push back, to which the Chair replied, "I can get another one of you tomorrow, but I can't get another Lewis".

There is a lovely parable that illustrates the value of experience and knowledge, the first version of which appeared on 1st February 1908 in *The Journal of the Society of Estate Clerks of Works*, by the "Hampshire Observer" printing works, Winchester. A later version goes like this:

> A ship's engine had failed. The ship's owners tried one expert after another, but none of them could fix the broken engine. Then they brought in a man who had been fixing ships since he was young. He carried a large bag of tools with him and immediately went to work. He inspected the engine very carefully, top to bottom. The old man reached into his bag and pulled out a

small hammer. He gently tapped something. Instantly, the engine lurched into life.

A week later, the owners received an invoice from the old man for $10,000. "What!" the owners exclaimed. "He hardly did anything!" So, they wrote to the man, "Please send us an itemised invoice".

The man sent an invoice that read:

Tapping with a hammer – $ 2.00

Knowing where to tap – $9,998.00

Again, the owners' greatest asset was being able to access the right information and knowledge at the right time.

In Chapter 2 we observed how the value of Information Assets is contextual. Different information will be of different value to different people at different times. So how do we determine which information is of what value, to whom and when? Answer, we ask them. A Reservoir Engineer or Geophysicist in an oil and gas producer knows exactly what data, information and knowledge is of value to them. They use those Information Assets every day. It is the same for somebody in HR, in the warehouse, in Finance and on the Board.

WHY WE NEED TO PUT INFORMATION ASSETS TO WORK: THE BUSINESS IMPACT

In Chapter 5 we examined the business impact of managing Information Assets well and putting them to work. In summary, the business impacts include the following.

1. **Mitigating business risk** which can encompass:
   a. compromised business continuity/succession;
   b. loss of personal and corporate reputation;
   c. loss of competitive advantage;
   d. inability to meet compliance obligations;
   e. inability to initiate or defend litigation; and
   f. inability to protect sensitive information, etc.
2. **Reducing operating cost.** Costs increase if you can't find the right information when you need it. There are plenty of examples in Chapter 5.

3. **Increasing value.** The value of the data, information and knowledge assets which can be monetised or have a market, book, replacement, deprival, social or other value.
4. **Deriving benefit** – the benefit to the organisation of managing Information Assets well, including;
   a. increased revenue;
   b. improved productivity;
   c. greater profitability;
   d. better, faster product and service provision;
   e. increased professionalism;
   f. heightened staff morale and satisfaction, etc.
5. **Operating in an ethical** manner. How we apply ethics to the management of Information Assets is becoming rapidly and increasingly important. How do we use Information Assets ethically to benefit humankind? And how do we maximise benefit whilst minimising harm?

WHAT IS REQUIRED TO PUT INFORMATION ASSETS TO WORK

You can put Information Assets to work if:

1. you know explicitly what the organisation does;
2. you know what data, information and knowledge is used by the organisation and for what purpose;
3. you know the value and sensitivity of those Information Assets and to whom;
4. you know what Information Assets to manage (because many are not worth managing) and how; and
5. your Information Assets are of high quality.

Examples

There are many examples of organisations that put their Information Assets to work effectively. In his latest book "Data Juice", Doug Laney refers to 101 of them. On the other hand, our research findings and anecdotal evidence have shown that many organisations are not exploiting their Information

Assets to improve business performance and create competitive advantage. The following examples show the impact of this.

Jeweller

The owner of an Adelaide-based jeweller visited one of his jewellery mates in Melbourne. He was asked, "How is the business going?" The owner told him. His mate said, "You could do better. When do you sell your biggest rocks?" The owner said, "I don't know".

So, the owner returned home and asked his Information Manager to find out. Which he did.

So, I ask you, what time of the day, on what day of the week does the jewellery store sell its biggest rocks? Is it at lunchtime on Wednesdays? Is it after work on Fridays? No, it is at 8:00 am on Monday mornings. Why? We can only surmise. Perhaps it has something to do with celebration or apology!

The owner began putting out his biggest rocks when people wanted to buy them. And the business boomed.

The point of this story is that it requires an understanding of the business, an appreciation of the importance of high-quality customer data and some simple analysis.

Law Firm

After completing an Information Asset Management Health Check including Business Impact Assessment, the Managing Partner of an Adelaide law firm noted that approximately 70% of their 150 fee earners could bill an additional 30 min per day and 20% could bill more than an extra hour per day, if the firm more effectively managed its Information Assets. They have therefore been operating very inefficiently up to that point. He declared,

> [Improving the management of our Information Assets] now represents our firm's single greatest source of competitive advantage, but if our current [inefficient] information management practices are disclosed [to our clients], we're toast.

This exercise required an understanding of the importance of billable hours to the firm's revenue and the sensitivity of clients to the firm's efficiency. It required some information about how much time was being wasted on poor Information Asset management practices.

Naval Shipbuilding

With global assistance Australia recently built three Air Warfare Destroyers. It is an age-old principle that you get better as you learn. It may be apocryphal, but the scuttlebutt, to use a naval term, is that Ship 2 was built at an approximately 40% lower cost than Ship 1 and Ship 3 was built at a further 30% lower cost than Ship 2. Why? Because we learnt how to build ships. We had the data, information, knowledge, experience and wisdom to drive those extraordinary cost reductions. If the Australian Navy can replicate that improvement across $200 billion worth of naval shipbuilding, we should be able to save around $60 billion, which is enough to fund the building of 20 new hospitals.

We need to know how to build ships, what Information Assets are valuable to whom, how to manage them efficiently and effectively, and how to get the right data, information and knowledge to the right people and the right time whilst protecting it from malicious actors.

The lesson from all these examples is: Organisations should understand that if they invest in the management of their Information Assets, they will help to mitigate their business risk, see a sizeable return on their investment and make them more competitive. It is important to note that we are not putting the boot into technology or IT professionals. The IT department is our valued business partner. However, we are calling into question the "wisdom" of thinking that "data is the new oil", and of abdicating the management and leveraging of the Information Assets to the IT department, who will inevitably rush out and buy a piece of technology or a bit of software, because that is precisely what you pay them to do.

- How does your organisation drive business performance by leveraging its Information Assets?

14

Why Is Justifying Investment in the Effective Management of Your Information Assets So Difficult?

INTRODUCTION

In Chapter 13 we:

- discussed how to determine your most valuable assets;
- discussed how data, documents, content and knowledge can be put to work and leveraged to mitigate risk, reduce costs, increase value, drive benefits and ensure ethical corporate behaviour;
- revisited what is required to establish the foundations from which Information Assets can be leveraged; and
- showed some simple case studies of how Information Assets have been put to work with significant, measurable, positive business impact.

In this chapter we will:

- describe the justification domain;
- show what good and bad look like;
- describe what a Justification Model is and does; and
- present the findings of our research into why it is so difficult to justify investment in improving Information Asset management practices.

EXECUTIVE OVERVIEW

A fundamental reason why organisations do not continuously invest in the improvement of their Information Asset management practices is that they

 DOI: 10.4324/9781003439141-14

do not have a model that allows justification of investment in the effective management of Information Assets. A Justification Model allows organisations to value and recognise non-financial benefits such as better decision-making, customer satisfaction, improved service delivery, compliance with your legislative and regulatory environment, and improved staff professionalism and morale. If investment in the governance and management of Information Assets can be justified, and if the quality of those Information Assets can be improved, the benefits enjoyed are many and varied. There are many different reasons why organisations find it difficult to justify investment in improving Information Asset management practices.[1]

DOMAIN 10: JUSTIFICATION

The justification domain assesses how the business case for information management initiatives is developed.

An ability to leverage and exploit Information Assets (Domain 9) demands the ability to recognise the business impact that ensues (Domain 10). The ability to recognise business impact (Domain 10) enables that impact to be quantified and articulated (Domain 1).

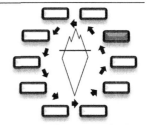

The justification domain informs the first domain, namely the business impacts domain. With an appropriate justification model, the benefits from effective Information Asset management can be crystallised and recognised.

WHAT GOOD AND BAD LOOK LIKE

For the justification domain, this is what good and bad look like:

What good looks like	Investment in the continuous improvement in the quality of Information Assets is justified on the basis of recognising both tangible and intangible benefits. The organisation's justification model allows these benefits to be identified. Maturity, value and benefits are regularly measured and recorded.

What bad looks like	Investment in management of Information Assets is based upon buying IT infrastructure. Business cases are built upon technical risk, for instance maintenance expiry or cyber exposure, and cost reduction, not upon the intangible benefits of productivity improvement, business risk mitigation, competitive advantage, service delivery or staff satisfaction. Investment is project, not continuous improvement oriented.

JUSTIFICATION MODEL

Our ultimate objective is to assist organisations to continuously invest in the improvement of their Information Asset management practices based upon the realisation and recognition of the benefits that ensue. Despite having had this objective for decades, and despite us being business advisers, researchers, lecturers and authors, we have comprehensively failed. We suspect that a fundamental reason for this is that organisations simply do not have a model that allows justification of investment in the effective management of Information Assets.

Earlier in this book we asked whether either actively (wrongdoing) or passively (neglect) deciding to sub-optimally manage the organisation's most valuable resource, its Information Assets, is the equivalent of deciding to manage the organisation badly. And we asked if deciding to manage the organisation badly is negligent. Surely it must be. And shareholders and taxpayers should be furious about this.

How can executives take pride or enjoyment in their work if all they want to do is put out bushfires? Where is the striving for excellence, for the improvement in outcomes for owners and customers and staff? For themselves? These are the people who fall into the "There is a problem, and the organisation is aware of it, but there is no interest in addressing it" state that we identified in the preface. As we said before, these people don't ask for help.

We must identify the following.

- What needs to be in place for sound investment decisions to be made?
- What would justify an investment in the management of the organisation's Information Assets?
- How are risks quantified so investment in mitigation can be justified?
- How are opportunities evaluated so investment in new initiatives can be justified?
- What creates a call to action? And a call to action now?

As we saw from Chapter 3, of all the findings of our research, the most frustrating and vexatious topic for boards and executives is how to justify investment in (the continuous improvement of) Information Asset quality. It attracted the largest number of comments over the broadest range of topics. If we can crack the justification nut, we will change the way Information Assets are governed and managed forever.

If investment in the governance and management of Information Assets can be justified, and if the quality of those Information Assets can be improved, the benefits enjoyed are many and varied. As we mentioned in Chapter 5, after improving the Information Asset management practices of a winery, an operations staff member said, "This is fantastic. We can now find stuff".

However, the accountants will say, "We are only interested in hard cost reductions, and you can't sack ten percent of a person".

A Justification Model allows organisations to value and recognise non-financial benefits. Depending on the organisation, these benefits may include, amongst other things, mitigated business risk, better decision-making, customer satisfaction, improved competitive advantage, increased productivity, faster and better product and service development, improved service delivery, compliance with your legislative and regulatory environment, and improved staff professionalism and morale. All these benefits are intangible, but real. They are in addition to reduced costs, increased revenue and higher profits.

Although government agencies must work to a budget, they are not profit-driven and are therefore concerned with more nebulous measurements like service delivery. Government agencies are also much more concerned about compliance. Compliance is an effective catalyst for improving Information Asset management, particularly recordkeeping, but it provides a very poor justification.

WHY ORGANISATIONS FIND IT HARD TO JUSTIFY INVESTMENTS IN INFORMATION ASSET MANAGEMENT

Our research has found that there are many reasons why organisations find it difficult to justify investment in improving Information Asset management practices, including the following.

There Is No Catalyst or Incentive to Act

Apart from the lack of awareness as discussed in Chapter 6, an important barrier is a lack of incentive to invest the time and effort into managing Information Assets. Ineffective and inefficient Information Asset Management does not necessarily stop a business from running, which decreases its priority and encourages complacency. Yesterday, as I write this, I had a coffee with a marketing expert. He said, "The problem you face is there is no crisis". A CEO (HR Services) commented that their Information Assets are not managed well, but it is not stopping them from making money. While they're making money, "it gets pushed out there into the future – one day, one day, we'll do these things". The bad management of Information Assets rarely causes an overt problem and the Managing Partner of an Australian law firm commented that "we didn't go broke, we didn't lose much value, the crisis never occurred". A Knowledge Manager and a Board member in the banking sector both commented that senior managers do not pay attention to data, information and knowledge because everything is working fine, and people can find what they need to do their jobs. The CKO added that businesses have insurance cover in case something happens, "so why worry?"

In organisations where the value of Information Assets is not recognised, it often takes a crisis or severe financial loss to change the attitude. The CFO of a financial institution confirmed that it sometimes takes a disaster "for example when you lose that key person and there are no procedures, there are no documents".

Compliance Requirements Are Often the Only Driver

Organisations must comply with various reporting authorities, and they must understand the laws and regulations and their impact on information management and internal control systems. The US Sarbanes–Oxley Act of 2002 is an example of such legislation. Unfortunately, organisations often seem to only pay attention to the management and governance of data, information and knowledge if they are forced to comply with regulations and legislation. The added focus on compliance has resulted in even more reluctance to manage information, and a Chief Information Officer (CIO) of a financial institution noted that "many employees save and keep all e-mails, files, data and information to ensure that they do not get into any kind of trouble". This leads to waste and legal repercussions, and the time and energy someone has to spend making sense of it are often not considered.

A large Australian Federal government agency with offices in 46 countries wanted to install an Electronic Document and Records Management System (EDRMS). We asked the Chief Information Officer (in reality, a Chief Technology Officer) how he was justifying the expenditure. He said, "I will invest until the agency is compliant, and I will invest not one cent more". Nothing was said about business outcomes.

A CIO of a Local Government agreed: "I think it's easier to sell the information benefits on the back of compliance". People see a secondary benefit in managing the information, "like it's going to keep me out of jail if I comply with the legislation". The CIO of the financial institution agreed that "the day they say to the finance guys that there are new Internal Financial Revenue Services (IFRS) rules, things will change overnight as far as managing the intangible assets are concerned".

Information Asset Management Gets Lost in the Day-to-Day Activities

The CFO of an Automotive Services organisation commented that the priority of managing Information Assets "tends to get pushed away" as "there are other priorities, a thousand priorities". He added that managers are too busy with day-to-day activities such as "putting out fires, making money, making the customer happy and putting aside five minutes a week to think about what we're going to do with our systems". The CEO of an HR Services company observed that this is especially true for organisations that are growing rapidly as, "they have more important issues, such as space issues and staffing issues that occupy more of my thinking than anything else". External pressure such as a volatile economic climate also impacts on the Information Asset management of businesses. The CEO of a large manufacturing firm said,

> We've just been through the GFC, and sales are tough, and business is tough. We've got a lot of immediate priorities to generate better cash flows and better returns to shareholder. You get locked up a bit in the here and now.

The Cost of Managing Information Assets Is Unknown

The cost of data, information and knowledge are often not recorded. Accounting standards do not allow organisations to determine these costs, or the costs are too difficult to determine. Identified costs usually relate to amounts associated with the acquisition, operation, and maintenance of an information system. None of the research participants indicated that cost associated with the time to interact with an Information Asset system to enter required data was determined. The CFO of the automotive services company agreed, "We do not cost and value our Information Assets as we should, but I think we are slowly waking up to that. But, is it getting the attention that it deserves? Yes, slowly. Is it top priority? No".

The cost of information is often unknown because it is intangible. The Data Manager of a large Australian bank commented,

> Show me a bucket of information. And if I did show you a bucket of information it would be a bunch of hard drives and well what's that worth? But, what's on those hard drives is a potentially measurable value to your organisation.

The Board member of a financial institution said:

> If you go and buy a new bulldozer, you know that bulldozer is going to last 15 years, and you know that it cost you $200 000, so you depreciate it over that period of time. It is very easy to understand, and you've got a return on that investment that's well quantified. The value of Information Assets is at best a guestimate in terms of derived revenue or customer value, which is why accountants have a hard time figuring it out.

The Value of Information Assets Is Unknown

Organisations don't spend enough time thinking about the value and importance of Information Assets. The CFO of the Automotive Services organisation observed,

> I understand that there is great value in the Information Assets and the sharing of information within the organisation. But, like all organisations, we certainly struggle with it, and we don't bring it to the surface and give it the level of resources that it would need to get that value out. I think if we did understand the value then we'd change our thinking.

This indicates a gap in people's understanding of what drives value and managers assume that these assets will still be there tomorrow. Organisations also do not have a way to measure the value of data, information and knowledge as the information is so widespread in email, Internet content, policies and procedures et cetera. A CFO of a financial institution said, "it's just wholesale across the business" and added that he does not know how people would go about capturing and valuing these assets and whether there is a reliable method to do it.

The Value of Data, Information and Knowledge Is Contextual

The value of data, information and knowledge is temporally, managerially and professionally contextual. In terms of time, the CEO of an HR Services firm said that "there's something ephemeral about the assets we have, if you can call them assets. Yesterday I had an asset. Today I have none. So, it's very, it's a very ephemeral asset to have". The value of data, information and knowledge is also contextual in terms of level in the organisation (level of seniority). The CIO of a financial institution is of the opinion that information must be interpreted at all the layers of the organisation, so it makes sense to the people at the junior levels. Finally, the value of data, information and knowledge is contextual in terms of functional areas in the business. Different groups and individuals have different views of information management. The CIO agreed that "the information challenges that you meet really depend on the area where you operate from".

The Value of Information Assets Cannot Be Determined Until a Business Is Sold

The CEO of the HR Services firm identified that a reason for the ineffective management of Information Assets is that the value of a business is only determined when the business is sold. The accounting system doesn't allow a business to value information on the balance sheet. Wilson and Stenson[2] are of the opinion that

> one can argue with some conviction that what is not shown on an enterprise's balance sheet (for example morale of employees, purchase pre-disposition in the marketplace, managerial capability, Information Assets) is of greater importance than that which is shown.

Goodwill is an intangible asset and "you can't put goodwill onto your balance sheet. You only put it on there when you buy somebody else's business".

Accounting Practices Do Not Account for Data, Information and Knowledge

Traditional accounting ratios have not been able to measure intangible assets. Participants in our research agreed that data, information and knowledge are of value to the company, but indicated that, under the accounting rules and various other traditional practices, they are not formally accounted for and reported on the balance sheet unless it is a substantial activity. None of the organisations we interviewed use ratios for measuring intellectual capital, e.g. knowledge ratio, return on knowledge assets or training expenses per employee. A possible explanation for why organisations do not use knowledge ratios is that anything that is considered an asset must be reflected by the organisations' end-of-year financial statements. Organisations with more knowledge workers would therefore have to pay more tax on their knowledge assets. The CEO of a manufacturing company observed that "if the accounting systems don't create the ability to value information, then businesses won't either".

The Benefits of Managing Information Assets Effectively Are Unknown

An important barrier to the introduction of Information Management into organisations is the poor recognition of its potential benefits. Senior managers rely on tangible experience and common sense, and it is therefore difficult to persuade them that formal information management leads to organisational success. The Manager of a financial institution said they focus on "hard things that make the business work, such as sales, getting the products to market, collecting and investing the money and making sure it gets onto the books, as well as managing expenses". The CIO of a financial institution noted that the focus of a young organisation is on growing more rapidly and initiatives that bring more business "rather than looking for benefits of intangibles". Investors are mostly concerned with the bottom line and are therefore focused on revenue and costs. Managers believe that they would be able to make better decisions and therefore show a return on investment if they had more high-quality information. The CFO of the Automotive Services organisation commented that "everybody in business understands they don't manage their Information Assets well, but they don't know what the benefit is by actually managing them a lot better". He added that their organisation had trouble justifying the investment in a data warehouse, as the business people could not see the benefit of using the data warehouse and commented:

> We're going to spend all this money, pushing the data to the one position and one access point, but am I going to be able to run the business any better? No one could see they could run the business any better, so the data warehouse sort of fell apart.

The Benefits from Managing Information Assets Well Are Intangible

The difficulty with Information Assets is the finite quantification of the benefits. Measuring the benefits of Information Assets is not easy. The CKO of a utilities company said that she couldn't find any hard benefits and "for the project to get off its legs at the time, I had to show hard benefits". The CIO of a financial institution agreed that it is extremely difficult to work at such a conceptual level because it requires "abstract or conceptual thinking". An interesting comment from the CFO of a financial institution was that Myers Briggs research shows that a good three-quarters of people are inherently sensing (S) and judging (J) people, who care about hard facts, concrete data and lack flexibility. He added that "most people don't like what is nebulous, which is why they struggle with these intangibles". The CKO of a Government department has the view that organisations are not good at measuring the benefit in dollar terms, but they can understand it "in reduction of pain". Measuring the benefits of tangible assets is easier and shareholders look at the dollar values of physical assets, physical liabilities and the generation of wealth. A Board member of a bank articulated it as follows: "You misappropriate $1 million, and it comes out. You lose a truck, everyone asks 'where's the truck?' But this is nebulous".

The Benefits from Managing Information Assets Well Are Intertwined

Information and knowledge only assume value when it affects decision-making and if it leads to action to benefit an organisation. It is hard to prove that you are managing information better than everybody else and put a value on that. The CEO of the manufacturing company observed that potential purchasers would want to do due diligence and expect the firm to show how they manage information better than anybody else.

If a business misses out on a job, they can see that clearly, but they cannot see the opportunity to make more profit on a job they did get. It is very hard to measure, and one would have to get inside the job and look at how people were working"

The Managing Partner of a law firm agreed, "Unless you are intimately involved you can't just pick up a piece of paper and tell that it was clearly done inefficiently".

Data, information and knowledge contribute value to the business to the extent that they are often the triggers of business processes. It is difficult to attribute value to the information itself – maybe it is the value of the transaction that it triggers. The CIO of a finance firm commented that he has difficulty trying to understand how he would value a piece of information coming in, in isolation of the whole business process. The CIO of a government organisation indicated that they are beginning to understand process, and to see the value of process. He said:

I have difficulty trying to understand how I would value a piece of information coming in, in isolation of the whole business process. Rather than saying we're going to drive it from an information perspective towards the process, we are driving from the process and information is popping out.

The Benefits from Managing Information Assets Well Are Difficult to Crystalise

Managers often believe that there is significant value in information, but the CFO of the automotive services organisation asked: "How do you wrap your arms around it and how do you give it value?" The problem goes back to CFOs who want to know how much it is costing them behind the scenes, but also how much more value they get out of the business by using Information Assets better. The cost and return on investment of an information and knowledge management programme therefore must be justified to the organisation's Board. Management teams usually want to know what the return in hard cash will be on their spending. This is often impossible, as knowledge is an intangible asset. The available models and measures of hard return on investment have yet to be accepted as a standard model in the world of information and knowledge management.

In Certain Service Industries It Pays to Be Inefficient

The drive for efficiency in certain industries is profit margin and the pricing model does not force them to minimise the time they spend doing a job. A Managing Partner of a law firm said that until lawyers are forced to operate efficiently, they are actually rewarded for being disorganised. "If I'm a lawyer, if it takes all day, that's all right. In fact, the longer it takes the better. There's not a huge incentive to get super organised across the firm". Effective information management is also not critical in the consulting business because they charge on a time and materials type basis. The CEO of an HR Services firm added, "So we're not always looking for the shortest route home".

Managing Information Assets Is Not Interesting

The management of information is not an interesting topic. The CKO of a Government department said: "It's a pretty dry topic. I don't think most people really want to think about it, because it's pretty difficult. It's not as tangible as hard assets like money". The CIO of a local government organisation agreed that "people do not read the information policy first thing in the morning. You don't see people thinking that it is a beautiful piece of information. It's a hard sell".

People Have Their Own Agendas

As discussed in Chapter 11 on Information Behaviour, one of the most important barriers to the implementation of information management is the adoption of a proprietary attitude to information on the part of certain individuals and departments. People look at information as power and they are therefore reluctant to share it with others. Self-interest (what's in it for me?) was also identified by the interview participants as a barrier. People have their own agendas and most people in organisations are only focused on survival. As a result, they do not drive the business and make the best decisions for the business. As the Chief Executive of an Information Services business said, "It's all about their own agenda".

Risk Management Is Seen as a Burden

As information is seen as a corporate asset, there are opportunities in managing it well and risks in managing it poorly. Organisations therefore need to understand where their risks lie and focus on managing their assets. This requires organisations to understand where their Information Assets are held, just as they need to understand where their money is. The important issues will be governance and clear accountabilities; cultural issues and staff training; capability of supporting professionals; clarity and appropriateness of processes and procedures and supporting technical infrastructure. The effective management of Information Assets therefore requires appropriate enabling systems and practices. Organisations seem to understand financial issues and know how to respond, but their understanding of information issues is weaker.

The CKO of a Utilities company agreed that it is sometimes necessary to "go down the risk route and start scaring them". Maybe the crisis hasn't happened, but some organisations face risks that "if we don't fix them, they can potentially become costly". The only way in which she was able to convince the organisation that they needed to focus on their records and information was to "go straight to the business risk guy and ask whether he realises the risks that the organisation faces, based on the fact that we're not managing our records and our information properly. That was the turning point, as he understood the risks".

Whilst the management of risk is clearly a business driver, it also requires effort and enterprises often see it as an administrative burden. Senior managers, who should be leading their organisations on a strategic level, often find that their days are being consumed with compliance activities. The CIO of Local government said, "You can see how frustrated he is, and he has actually become quite aggressive about it".

Justification: On a Positive Note

Some organisations reported that they derived benefits from managing their Information Assets. It was interesting that the Manager of a financial services company indicated that he wasn't actually interested in doing benefits analysis, as the benefits were obvious and that he does not want to

> waste valuable resource time on justifying what is completely obvious anyway. Just by walking around the organisation I can see how people use the system and how they can collaborate and work more effectively. I know the benefits have been realised because people are using the system on an every-minute-of-the-day basis.

In another organisation the benefits were also visible, and the Manager commented that the success has been exponential; "success breeds success". As soon as people started gaining value out of the Information Assets, they are very quick to find other opportunities within their immediate business environment, and then it starts snowballing.

The Chief Knowledge Officer of a utilities company agrees:

> Instead of quantifying it from a hard benefit, I prefer to show and communicate back the success stories. That's how I try to prove value to the organisation. So, every time I hear that somebody saved some time by accessing a document that they didn't have to redo themselves, or finding a specialist really quickly on the intranet, or using one of our external research tools to learn more about a client, I capture and communicate it back to the business.

Many years ago, we were asked by an energy provider in Queensland to assist with developing a business case to justify the purchase and implementation of an Electronic Document and Records Management System (EDRMS). Three times the organisation had tried and three times it had failed. With our help, the fourth attempt was successful, and we were delighted. In our naivety we breathlessly asked,

> What are you going to do with the business case?
> Nothing.
> What!?
> Nothing.
> But you have spent all this money and we have spent all this time.
> What you have helped us to understand is the real reason for doing this. We have too many people spending too much time doing things inefficiently. The result is people are working too hard and there is too much unpaid overtime being worked. We just want them to go home to their families on time.

Brilliant. And when it came to the management of the cultural change associated with the purchase and implementation of the EDRMS, how hard would that have been to sell?

- How does your justification model deal with intangible benefits?
- How does your organisation justify investment in Information Asset management initiatives?
- How does your organisation fund the management of its Information Assets? Is it:
  - o done on the basis of IT infrastructure projects?;
  - o funded by the business, for the business, based on the measured benefits driven by the continuous improvement in the quality of its Information Assets?; or
  - o other?
- How does your organisation fund the continuous improvement in the quality of its Information Assets?

NOTES

1. Evans, N., & Price, J. 2014. Why Organisations Cannot Justify the Effective Management of Their Information Assets. *European Conference of Management, Leadership and Governance (ECMLG),* Zagreb, Croatia. 13–14 November.
2. Wilson, R. M. S., & Stenson, J. A. (2008). Valuation of Information Assets on the Balance Sheet: The Recognition and Approaches to the Valuation of Intangible Assets. *Business Information Review,* .

15

How Does the Effective Management of Your Information Assets Support the Digital Transformation of Your Organisation?

INTRODUCTION

In Chapter 14 we:

- described the justification domain;
- showed what good and bad look like;
- described what a Justification Model is and does; and
- presented the findings of our research into why it is so difficult to justify investment in improving Information Asset management practices.

In this chapter we will discuss:

- the need for digital business transformation;
- misconceptions about digital business transformation;
- the effect of the COVID-19 pandemic; and
- the important link between digital business transformation and the management of your Information Assets.

EXECUTIVE OVERVIEW

Now that we have finished discussing each of the ten domains, let's consider the overall topics that affect the management of your Information Assets. The

DOI: 10.4324/9781003439141-15

competitive dynamics of modern organisations have changed significantly over the past few years. Technological advancement has resulted in changing expectations of customers. To take advantage of the capabilities of the new technologies and satisfy the requirements of customers and clients, enterprises are forced to completely transform themselves. Businesses integrate digital technology into all aspects of the business to fundamentally change the way a business operates, creates value and interacts with stakeholders such as customers, employees and partners.

A digital business transformation requires the ability to access, analyse and use information in real-time to make better decisions, improve customer experiences and increase the speed of innovation. Information is therefore at the heart of every digital transformation, and the art of managing it efficiently and securely is the challenge.

Organisations that do not digitally transform will not survive. They will die a natural death, starved of revenue and talent. A key message of this book is that, without the absolute commitment and determination of business executives, both the effective management of the Information Assets and the digital transformation of the organisation, will fail. It is essential to take time to reflect and learn from mistakes, learn from successes and use that as input for the next step.

The COVID-19 crisis has highlighted the urgency for customer centricity and frictionless business. These business attributes are only enabled by digital business transformation. Digital business transformation requires effective Information Asset management. And that in turn requires managing data, information and knowledge as a valuable resource and as a strategic business asset. It requires managing Information Assets the way financial assets are managed.

A HOLISTIC VIEW OF DIGITAL BUSINESS TRANSFORMATION

While a large body of research on digital business transformation exists, few people have holistically explored all the facets of the transformation of the whole business, which includes a new digital business transformation strategy, the need for different leadership styles and staff competencies, improvements in business models, improved customer experiences and seizing business opportunities by taking advantage of the changes and opportunities offered by digital technologies. In this book we adopt the term *digital business transformation*, to emphasise that the focus is on the transformation of the business, not on the "digital" (or technology) aspect. One can also use the term "digital enterprise transformation" in the context of large organisations.[1,2]

Digital business transformation differs from other initiatives such as continuous process improvement, new product installation and digitalisation where the focus is on implementing emerging technologies to enhance process efficiency and productivity. Digital business transformation is not equal to digitisation or digitalisation; it is more than pushing bits of paper through a scanner. Digital business transformation fundamentally changes organisations' traditional ways of doing business. A transformation is messy, disruptive and exceptionally difficult to implement and therefore it requires a holistic approach and genuine executive commitment to succeed.

Let's be specific for a moment. *Digitisation* is converting information from analogue to digital, i.e. converting ink-on-paper records to digital computer files. Digital data are exponentially more efficient than analogue, but business systems and processes are still largely designed around analogue-era ideas about how to find, share and use information. *Digitalisation* is using digitised information to make established ways of working simpler and more efficient. Digitalisation isn't about changing how you do business or create new types of businesses. It's about keeping on doing what you've always done, but faster and better now that the data is instantly accessible. *Digital transformation* is about changing the way business gets done and, in some cases, creating entirely new classes of businesses. Organisations revisit everything they do, from internal systems to customer interactions both online and in person. This leads to better decision-making, game-changing efficiencies and a better customer experience.

WHAT DRIVES DIGITAL BUSINESS TRANSFORMATION?

Digital transformation is high on the list of priorities for organisations feeling the pressure to adapt to the changing environment. Digital business transformation is driven by many factors, for example:

1. Customers are more entitled and demanding, and they need to be more effectively engaged at every touchpoint in the customer experience lifecycle. Stakeholders have more information than ever before, and they expect instant digital feedback be provided about products, services, partners and customers. Stakeholders are too well informed to tolerate ineffective and inefficient operations: business owners demand higher returns, lower risk and improved competitive advantage; clients demand customer centricity and frictionless business where higher quality goods and services are delivered faster and cheaper; and suppliers and staff demand faster, easier processes and improved decision-making. Digital business transformation closes the gap between what digital customers expect and what existing businesses can deliver.
2. Advancements in technology are allowing much larger quantities of data and information to be processed and the digital world allows benefits such as lower costs, higher efficiency and innovation to be realised at the same time.
3. Start-ups can threaten businesses and entire industries and new skills will be required of managers and employees.

The COVID-19 pandemic increased the urgency for businesses to transform by accelerating the shift to digital and fundamentally shaking up the business landscape. McKinsey[3] observes that

> the shutdowns or slowdowns in business and consumer activity, as well as closures of physical workplaces have given many companies the "kick in the pants" they needed to speed up their pace of digital transformation on a scale not seen since wartime.

Digital business transformation initiatives exploded as enterprises realised that there was no alternative, besides improving their digital capabilities to compete better in the marketplace. The pandemic has accelerated digital adoption across all industries, including retail, education and healthcare, in many cases making business' previous strategies obsolete in a matter of weeks.

Daragh OBrien asserts that

> most of what has been done as Digital Transformation in the last 20 years has been sticking lipstick on a pig. However, the global COVID-19 crisis has shone an unfavourable light on the gaps and the sticking plasters passing for strategy.

MISCONCEPTIONS ABOUT DIGITAL
BUSINESS TRANSFORMATION

There seem to be many misconceptions regarding the nature of digital business transformation. People often believe that digital business transformation and digitalisation are the same, that it is led and owned by the Chief Information Officer or Chief Digital Officer, and that the focus is all about technology. Given that digital technologies cause business disruptions and challenges, they believe that business solutions also lie in digital technologies. This misconception is referred to as the "technology fallacy".[4]

Laura Sebastian-Coleman says that most organisations reach for an IT solution and skip information quality when addressing the spectre of cybersecurity threats:

> Even though the term digital transformation has been around for a while, it is mostly a set of assertions that focus on technology, rather than information. Most come from vendors, so that is not surprising. These assertions emphasise that digital technologies create opportunities for people to interact differently. Yet they skip the part about the quality of the information. Organisations also skip the "transformation" part of digital transformation. If organisations are on a journey, that journey feels more like an adoption journey ("Hey! Let's get this cool new technology in place"), rather than a transformation journey ("Hey! We could take advantage of the information we can get through this technology and actually change how we work and interact with our customers"). People have confused technology and "shiny things" with meaningful change in the management and curation of the asset class. New bottles, but the wine is still vinegar. "Techno-fetishism" has therefore helped create this problem (we have an app for that), but it's through the wiser use of technologies to empower and enable people that we can help fix this.

Further misconceptions that occur amongst many academics and practitioners are that digital business transformation is an isolated, one-off project that follows a traditional approach and requires firm-wide change; that most businesses already have a good digital strategy; that it is a separate "thing" that is added to the existing business model; and that employees will accept the transformation without resistance.[5]

INFORMATION MANAGEMENT IS THE FOUNDATION OF DIGITAL BUSINESS TRANSFORMATION

According to a Boston Consulting group study, 70% of digital transformation projects fail. According to the study the failure often ties back to data and information; poor data and information quality and not having the right information in the right place. Information is the lifeblood of every business and the ability to use that information is critical for competitive advantage. As we said before, one of the key aspects of digital business transformation is the underlying fact that information is an asset. Information Assets – data, documents, online content and knowledge – are of critical business value. Information is, arguably, the greatest asset from a business perspective. Enterprises must manage information like the asset it is.[6,7]

As part of any digital transformation, organisations will naturally generate more data, information and knowledge than ever, from various sources. Digital technologies allow organisations to collect, store, manage and analyse data, which in turn enables organisations to gain insights, make data-driven decisions and improve customer engagement. Legacy information systems are highly unlikely to be up to the task of collecting, managing, securing and providing access to the Information Assets. In the previous chapters we described how our research found that Information Assets are (i) valuable; (ii) not managed well; (iii) incur risks and inefficiencies when they are managed badly; and (iv) drive significant business benefits when managed well. Every organisation in the digital age is a "digital business", and its information is its digital currency. Every organisation is information dependent; it's like gravity – you can't get away from it. Organisations are increasingly sourcing their IT strategically to provide flexibility, scalability and cost reductions. Furthermore, managing information strategically can mitigate business risk and drive business productivity and performance. A CFO in a financial institution said:

> The evidence is stacking up that you need to become data driven, information driven. Otherwise, you might as well pack up shop because there's going to be someone smarter, faster and quicker than you that's going to come along and take away your business.

Traditional information management methods are struggling to keep up with the constant and increasing stream of data and information coming into organisations. The links between digital transformation and "information" therefore most often relate to the Internet of Things (IoT) and Big Data (analytics). Daragh OBrien commented:

> We have allowed "Big Data" to become "Morbidly Obese Data" because there is a confusion between quantity and quality.

Various authors[8,9] agree that data, information and knowledge support every digital business transformation goal, namely:

- **Customer-centricity**, i.e. offering the best information and/or gaining the right insights to serve customers' needs. Organisations must capture the ever-rising amounts and types of data submitted by customers through various channels, to become fully *digital on the outside*.
- **Operational excellence**, i.e. enterprises are also concerned with internal efficiency and advances in operational excellence (*digital on the inside*). Operations and processes can only be improved by having the proper information and data to do so. This requires new systems that transform digital operations, streamline internal processes and manage the information overload to ensure proper governance and accessibility.
- **Developing effective knowledge workers** who can work with knowledge and know where that knowledge comes from and how it can be stored, shared, secured and leveraged.
- **Innovation** where information is key to achieving this digital transformation goal.
- **Employee satisfaction:** The ability of employees to utilise data, information and knowledge is what drives the business forward. Information management affects businesses on many levels, such as employee satisfaction and retention, risk mitigation, productivity and profit margins.
- **Ecosystems:** The success or failure of digital transformation fundamentally rests upon relationships with customers, employees and partners, i.e. information is the glue that enables disparate parts of the ecosystem to work together.

Information management therefore is, and should be, the cornerstone of any digital transformation strategy. Your future as an organisation depends on your ability to leverage this asset called information to gain a competitive edge in your industry. At the heart of every digital transformation initiative is accurate and up-to-date information. Without this, knowledge workers will not have the right information to work efficiently, and decision-making will not be optimised.

ADVANTAGES OF COMBINING EFFECTIVE INFORMATION ASSET MANAGEMENT AND DIGITAL BUSINESS TRANSFORMATION FOR YOUR ORGANISATION

The benefits of merging information management directly with the digital transformation strategy include:

1. **A single source of truth/single system of record**

   Organisations must be able to make sense of the content being managed, else the data can become lost and unusable. Organisations therefore need a system that lets workers access and leverage information that resides in any system or repository regardless of where the data is stored. They need a "single source of truth" to make informed business decisions.

2. **The right information to the right users at the right time**

   With data growing in complexity and scale, it is essential to have the necessary permissions in place to protect data and ensure that only authorised users can access, edit, move or delete it. These permissions should be automatically updated when employees leave or move into new roles to prevent unauthorised access at any time, to create a seamless transition across the workforce without the risk of sensitive information falling in the wrong hands.

3. **Improving operational efficiency**

   Automating manual processes can free up employees to focus on value-adding tasks and provide more control over workflows and data. Automated processes can operate continuously to ensure work is done on time and customers and other stakeholders are satisfied.

4. **Improving collaboration**

   While there are many benefits to remote working, productive collaboration can be difficult without face-to-face interaction. Many different types of intelligent collaboration software (e.g. Google Workspace, Trello, Slack, Zoom, Salesforce) facilitate real-time information sharing, eliminate version control issues and dropped email attachments and provide everyone with the most accurate and recent information. However, these tools are only as good as the change management, adoption and processes for using them. Implementing these tools without the complete package is just like installing Enterprise Resource Planning software without good information management.

5. **Compliance**

When it comes to keeping up with audits and compliance, information management systems can easily control user access using metadata and automatically ensure version control. It also maintains a clear audit trail for compliance and protects sensitive information (Smith, 2016).

6. **Future innovation**

Implementing intelligent systems provides a base for future innovation. Analytics, machine learning and artificial intelligence will all be critical for organisations to maximise the value of their information and data. As technologies continue to evolve and offer new opportunities, businesses must remain open to the possibilities and include them in their digital transformation strategy (Smith, 2016).

NOTES

1. Evans, N., Miklosik, A., Bosua, R., & Qureshi, A.M.A. 2022. Digital Business Transformation: An Experience-Based Holistic Framework. *IEEE Access*, 10: 121930–121939.
2. Zeelie, L., & Evans, N. 2021. Embarking on a Digital Enterprise Transformation Journey: Guiding Principles for Leaders. ECMLG, Online conference, November.
3. McKinsey. 2018. Digital Reinvention: Unlocking the 'How'. Digital/McKinsey, January 2018. Available at: https://www.mckinsey.com/business-functions/mckinsey -digital/our-insights/digital-reinvention-unlocking-the-how.
4. Kane, G.C., Nguyen Phillips, A., Copulsky, J.R., & Andrus, G.R. 2019. The Technology Fallacy—How People Are the Real Key to Digital Transformation. *MIT Sloan Management Review*. The MIT Press.
5. Evans, N., Miklosik, A., Bosua, R., & Qureshi, A.M.A. Digital Business Transformation: An Experience-Based Holistic Framework. *IEEE Access*, 10, 121930–121939.
6. Evans, N., & Price. J. 2012. Barriers to the Effective Deployment of Information Assets: An Executive Management Perspective. *Interdisciplinary Journal of Information and Knowledge Management (IJIKM)*, 7: 177–199

7. Laney, Douglas B. 2017. *Infonomics: How to Monetize, Manage, and Measure Information As an Asset for Competitive Advantage*, Taylor & Francis Group. *ProQuest Ebook Central*. Available at: https://ebookcentral.proquest.com/lib/unisa/detail.action?docID=5023889.

8. i-SCOOP. 2019. Digital Transformation and Information Management: Enabling Change, Conference in Digital Health (Rewiring Health). Available at: https://www.i-scoop.eu/digital-transformation/digital-transformation-and-information-management-enabling-change/.

9. Smith, D. 2016. Information Management Is Critical to Digital Transformation. idm. Available at: https://www.idm.net.au/article/0011210-information-management-critical-digital-transformation.

16

What You Can Do

INTRODUCTION

In Chapter 15 we discussed:

- the effect of the COVID-19 pandemic;
- misconceptions about digital business transformation;
- the important link between digital business transformation and the management of your Information Assets;
- the need for digital business transformation; and
- the advantages of the effective management of Information Assets and digital business transformation.

In this chapter we:

- summarise, at a very high level, what have discussed so far;
- will show you what you can do; and
- encourage you to act.

EXECUTIVE OVERVIEW

Organisations can take steps to improve the management of their Information Assets. They must not rely exclusively on traditional information technology solutions, but recognise that their data, information and knowledge comprise a strategic business asset that needs to be managed with the same diligence and rigour as that with which they manage their financial assets. Executives can use the Holistic Information Asset Management Model, which this book is based on, to guide improvement of Information Asset management practices. This in turn will enable their organisations to transform themselves for the digital era, mitigate their business risk, to be more competitive and profitable, improve business performance and enhance the customer or client experience.

HOW IMPORTANT ARE YOUR INFORMATION ASSETS?

Information Assets have become crucial for organisations' competitiveness and growth in the digital economy where organisations need to radically change how they operate and deliver value to their customers and clients.[1] Boards and senior management are well-versed in taking good care of the physical, financial and human assets, yet our research finds, and supports other literature, that hardly any mechanisms are in place for the management of Information Assets. Governance structures are rarely in place with a single Chief Information Officer who is not only responsible but also accountable for how that information is managed. As such, business governance structures rarely exist with a single person being accountable for the quality of the organisation's Information Assets. Given that money and information are both acknowledged as vital corporate assets, it is important to know why information is managed differently at enterprise level.

Many organisations do not have a precise and accurate description of their unique activity and they often do not know what data, documents, content and knowledge are deployed in the conduct of those activities. In many organisations, individuals manage their own information, and few people know where critical information can be found, who can access it and for how long it should be kept. Whilst they recognise that data, information and knowledge are vital to their operation, organisations do not know how to identify and manage the risk, cost, value, benefits and ethics associated with their Information Assets. Many organisations regard the cost of managing data, information and knowledge as equivalent to the combined cost of hardware, software, maintenance, support, upgrades, telecommunications and IT staff salaries, i.e. the cost of procuring and managing the infrastructure, but they do not consider the time that is spent managing information. Firms need to implement appropriate business management tools and solutions that are both effective and easy to use. Organisations should also implement a formal benefits realisation programme to measure the return on investment of their Information Asset management initiatives.

Every single individual in every organisation deals with data, information and knowledge almost every minute of every day, in reports, e-mails, spreadsheets, published content and business conversations. Changing behaviour and improving information practices are imperative. To manage their Information Assets effectively, organisations need to imbue a culture of valuing and managing data, information and knowledge by, amongst other initiatives, providing incentives and rewards to manage information as an enterprise resource to drive business performance and competitive advantage. Although every employee must take responsibility for managing information well, someone needs to be held accountable for the management of the organisation's Information Assets.

Digital business transformation utterly relies on good Information Asset management.[2]

> If information management is driving digital transformation and digital transformation requires better information management, then before enterprises implement a digital transformation strategy, they need to get their information management strategy in place too. Without it, they face failure.

SUMMARY

In summary:

1. Most organisations exist to deliver value to their owners whether they be citizens or shareholders.
2. They deliver value to their owners by delivering the right products and services to their customers at the right time for the right price.
3. Products and services are created for and delivered to customers through the activities of the organisation.
4. The activities of the organisation are enabled by the deployment of its resources.
5. An organisation has only four deployable resources – its Financial Assets (money), its Physical Assets (property and infrastructure), its

Human Assets (people) and its Intangible Assets (relationship capital, brand awareness, goodwill and data, information and knowledge).

6. Associated with these assets are risk, cost, value, benefit and ethics. They need to be managed well.

7. The most successful organisations are those that deliver the greatest value to their customers whilst consuming the fewest of their scarce and valuable resources.

8. Governance provides oversight and control over the management of the organisation and how resources are being deployed.

9. Directors and Board members, who govern organisations, must dictate who makes what asset management decisions. They need to know what questions to ask to determine whether the organisation's assets are being governed and managed well.

10. Contrary to conventional, accounting-based "wisdom", the job of management is not to drive business performance. Management's job is to deploy the resources of the organisation in the most efficient and effective manner possible. If they are, then business performance will follow. Business performance is a lag, not a lead, indicator of good business management.

11. Information Assets are arguably the organisation's most valuable. No business activity, no business process and no business decision can be conducted or made without the right data, information and/or knowledge. Not convinced? Think of what your organisation would be worth with no industry or business understanding, no customer data, no order, inventory or production data, no intellectual property, no financial information and no contracts.

12. Typically, an organisation's most valuable asset remains ungoverned and unmanaged. At every Board meeting, every month, the directors ask to see the organisation's Financial Statements. Yet, they don't even know what Information Statements are. An inability or unwillingness to properly govern the organisation's Information Assets is tantamount to negligence.

13. Directors and Board members must impose accountability on a single person for the management and deployment of the organisation's assets and resources. If they don't, nobody will care because it's not their job. This is clearly understood for Financial Assets in that a Chief Financial Officer (CFO) is genuinely accountable for the management of the organisation's Financial Assets. If the CFO mismanages the money (s)

he will be sacked and if they misappropriate the money, they will be jailed. There is true accountability around the management of Financial Assets, but less so for the others.

14. Typically, there is no accountability for the management and quality of the organisation's Information Assets.

15. Because their job and reputation depend upon it, the accountable person will naturally impose the corporate discipline required to manage Information Assets well.

16. Information Asset management is a business, not an IT, issue. Most organisations give responsibility to the mob that has "Information" in its title, ignoring what IT is measured on. As Tom Redman says, "Take data out of IT and do it this afternoon". As we mentioned, the Chief Executive of large American health business said, "I have invested in technology to the point where I can receive crap – at the speed of light".

17. Data, information and knowledge are only an asset if the right information can be found by the right people at the right time. If Information Assets cannot be found and used, they instantly become a liability. The asset needs to be of high quality, not crap.

18. Finding information requires knowing what it's been called and where it's been put, although advances in technology including Artificial Intelligence are making inroads here.

19. Naming and filing stuff require corporate discipline.

20. Corporate discipline requires principles, frameworks, tools, measurements, performance indicators, incentives and good leadership, management and staff behaviours.

21. Corporate discipline is cultural.

22. Culture requires careful communication.

23. Setting up the systems to support the corporate discipline and to facilitate naming and filing stuff requires human judgement. There is no system in the world that you can install, have it run around the organisation and tell you what the organisation does, what Information Assets it uses, which of those Information Assets are critical, who creates, captures, owns and uses these assets for what purpose, and where to find them. Organisations must stop being distracted by the shiny things. There is no silver bullet; instead, management needs to bite the bullet and impose the corporate discipline required.

24. The systems we set up need to be easy to use. If they are not, people will just find workarounds to the systems resulting in duplication of

information, no single source of truth or system of record, information chaos, and increasing liabilities and risk.

25. Sustaining good Information Asset management requires continuous improvement;

26. Continuous improvement requires funding.

27. Funding of continuous improvement requires understanding the risk, cost, value, benefit and ethics associated with those assets. No Chief Financial Officer worth his or her salt is going to even look at a business case if they don't perceive a problem to be solved, they won't approve the business case if they can't see the benefit and they won't reinvest if those benefits aren't crystallised, measured and reported.

RECOMMENDATIONS: WHAT TO DO

From the findings of our research and our decades of anecdotal evidence, we strongly recommend that you and your organisation:

1. support the foundations for digital business transformation by applying the Holistic Information Asset Management Model to:
   a. consider the maturity of your organisation's Information Asset management practices in line with the Model's ten domains. This provides a solid place from which to start; and
   b. guide the development of a roadmap to deliver tangible and measurable benefit, both to individuals and to the organisation (Domain 1).
2. educate the executive team about information as a valuable business asset (Domain 2);
3. impose through the board effective business governance over the management of the organisation's Information Assets, by making a single person ultimately accountable for managing this vital business asset (Domain 3);
4. show effective leadership and management of Information Assets by designing a vision of the future, imposing key performance indicators on the accurate and timely provision of information and developing

and implementing incentives and rewards for good information management behaviour (Domain 4);

5. interpret the business environment (Domain 3) in terms of Information Asset governance, ownership, strategy, principles, policy and work instructions, security and privacy, and the instruments required to manage the organisation's Information Assets (Domain 5);

6. ensure appropriate hardware, software and networks are in place to efficiently and deliver the right information to the right people at the right time (Domain 6);

7. develop and implement a behavioural change strategy and plan to educate all groups about the importance of managing Information Assets well and the benefits of doing so (Domain 7);

8. measure and improve the quality of its data, information and knowledge (Domain 8);

9. put the organisation's Information Assets to work to drive business outcomes and identify further opportunities (Domain 9);

10. develop and implement a justification model to enable intangible benefits to be recognised and continuous investment in the quality of the organisation's Information Assets to be justified (Domain 10); and

11. drive digital business transformation by a dedicated team that takes a holistic approach to transform the entire company. Business transformation is not a project or activity that can be delegated to the CIO/CTO or CMO in isolation.

By undertaking these steps appropriately organisations will improve the management of their Information Assets. The authors caution organisations not to rely exclusively on traditional information technology solutions, but to recognise that their data, information and knowledge comprise a strategic business asset that needs to be managed with the same diligence and rigour as that with which they manage their financial assets. The Holistic Information Asset Management Model is useful for guiding the improvement of Information Asset management practices. This in turn will enable organisations to transform themselves for the digital era, mitigate their business risk, to be more competitive and profitable, improve business performance and enhance the customer/client experience.

RECOMMENDATIONS: WHAT NOT TO DO

Do not:

- fail to make somebody truly accountable for the quality of the organisation's Information Assets;
- abdicate the responsibility for the management of Information Assets to IT. They don't own the assets, they don't understand the assets and they are not paid to manage the assets. Do not set IT up for failure; it's simply unfair;
- buy a silver bullet in the form of a technology solution. Bite the bullet and govern and manage your data, information and knowledge as the critical asset it is;
- fail to understand that the management of Information Assets is everybody's responsibility. Data, information and knowledge touch the lives of, and are used by, every single person in an organisation in every business decision, every business activity and every business process; and
- try to do all this yourself. Do not reinvent the wheel. There are genuine experts around the world who, for decades, have been crying out for board members, directors and executives to pay attention to their most vital business asset. We are not here to tell you that you have a problem. We are here to help you fix it.

RESOURCES AVAILABLE

Some of the best minds in the world volunteer their brilliance and the scars earned from their decades of experience to the Data Leaders www.dataleaders .org. Get in touch; we are more than happy to help.

Have a look at www.experiencematters.com.au. There is a wealth of information available on the website.

Or you can find us at:

James Price	Associate Professor Nina Evans
Managing Director, Experience Matters	*Professorial Lead, UniSA:STEM, University of South Australia*
☎ +61 (0) 438 429 144	☎ +61 (0) 420 831 331
✉ *james.price@experiencematters.com.au*	✉ *nina.evans@unisa.edu.au*
in https://www.linkedin.com/in/james-price-10741a4/	in https://www.linkedin.com/in/nina-evans-1b63965/
💻 *experiencematters.com.au*	💻 https://people.unisa.edu.au/Nina.Evans

NOTES

1. i-SCOOP. 2019. *Digital Transformation and Information Management: Enabling Change.* Conference in Digital Health.
2. Roe, D. 2019. *Why Information Management Plays a Critical Role in Digital Transformation.* CMS Wire.

Index

Printed in the United States
by Baker & Taylor Publisher Services